Viewing San Francisco's Coit Tower from a cable car

1,000 seals at Fisherman's Wharf, San Francisco

WHAT *you* WILL SEE

The 500-year-old Lone Cypress,
17-Mile Drive, Monterey Peninsula

Carmel Mission, founded in 1770
by Franciscan, Junipero Serra

Spectacular Yosemite Valley

Half Dome, Yosemite's icon

WHAT *you* WILL SEE

Main Street, Columbia State Historic Park

St. James Episcopal Church, circa 1860, Sonora

Emerald Bay from Inspiration Point, Lake Tahoe

Aboard the paddlewheeler, Tahoe Queen, Lake Tahoe

WHAT *you* WILL SEE

Pony Express Monument in historic Old Sacramento

Sutter's Fort, Sacramento

Sterling's vineyard, Napa Valley

Wine tasting at Chateau Souverain, Alexander Valley

Big Sur Coast, south of Carmel

Point Arena Light House, north of San Francisco

Let's Go to Northern California!

- **San Francisco, Monterey and Carmel, Yosemite, Gold Country, Lake Tahoe, Napa Valley...all are legendary for their natural beauty and charm.** Each is a vacation destination in itself. In seven days and 980 miles you can experience them all. But be forewarned: you'll want to go back for more.
- **As long-time residents of Northern California, we often visited and enjoyed these very special places.** In this book, we've researched and planned a driving tour that we would want to take ourselves if this were our first vacation in the State. So, let us be your guides; we'd like to share our expertise with you.
- **What's the best time to tour Northern California?** The weather is also legendary, so almost any time is good. However, late spring or early fall is best; you'll miss most of the coastal fog, most of the Central Valley heat, most of the mountain snow, and most of the crowds.
- **What if you don't have seven days?** See the section on Maps and Tour Options, where we outline two four-day tours. Do you have fourteen days? That's easy: stay an extra day in each location and enjoy the alternative activities we've listed.
- **Where will you eat and sleep?** To be honest, we've visited many of the accommodations and restaurants we list here, but not all. Those we haven't are consensus recommendations by trustworthy local residents or innkeepers, by the American Automobile Association or Mobil guides, or by Woodall's (for campgrounds). We strongly recommend reservations, especially if you plan to spend the night in Yosemite Valley or in the Wine Country. If you prefer different foods or price ranges than those we've listed, simply ask your innkeeper or front desk person for recommendations.
- **What's it likely to cost?** If you keep your lodging, food and car choices in the moderate range, two people should be able to take this tour for $2,000-$2,200. That will include accommodations, food, car rental, gasoline, entrance fees, pet kenneling, and film developing, but not transportation to California.
- **What else should you know?** The tour has been carefully pre-tested, so all you need to do is get in the car and follow this book. But there are some other things you may want to know before you go; you'll find them in the appendices. *There are links to most attractions and establishments at www.pridepublications.com.*

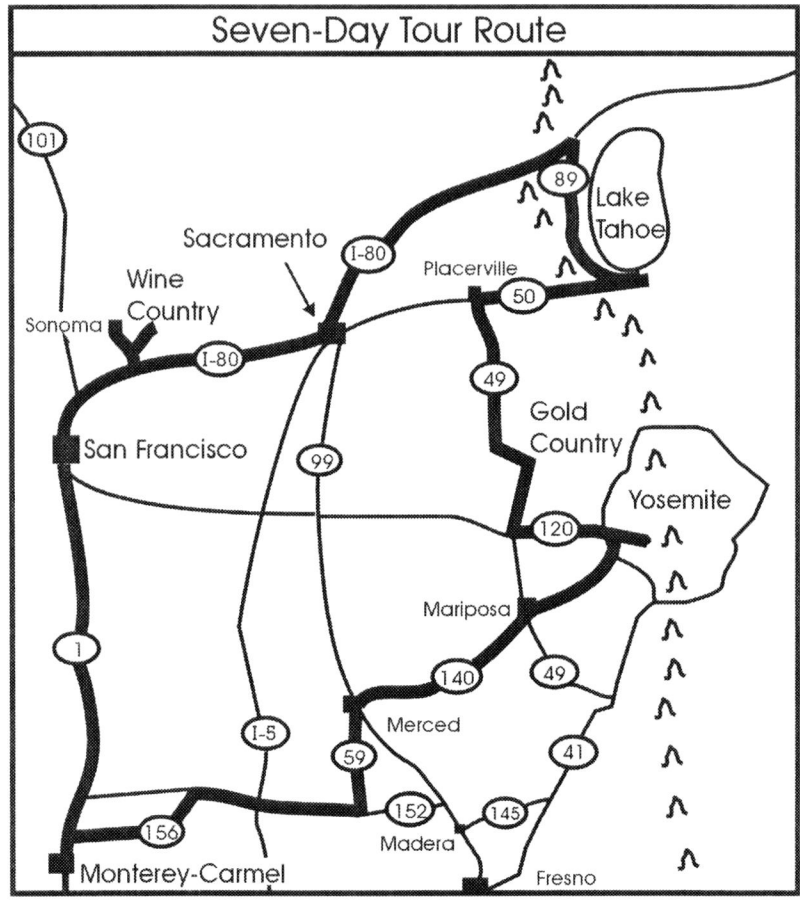

Visit and enjoy these attractions during *your* guided driving tour:

- **San Francisco**
- **Monterey and Carmel**
- **Yosemite National Park**
- **The Gold Country**
- **Lake Tahoe**
- **Historic Sacramento and Sonoma**
- **The Wine Country**

Seven Perfect Days™ Series

Seven Perfect Days™
in
Northern California

A Guided Driving Tour

by Bill and Celia Ginnodo

Arlington Heights, Illinois

* *

Seven Perfect Days™ *in Northern California*: *A Guided Driving Tour.* Text, maps and photographs copyright © 2007 by Pride Publications, Inc., 4 N. Wilshire Lane, Arlington Heights, IL 60004; tel 847-398-6212, fax 847-398-0670, e-mail *ginnodo@pridepublications.com*, website *www.pridepublications.com*.

Every effort has been made to provide accurate and up-to-date descriptions in this book. Hazards are noted where known. Users of this book are reminded that they alone are responsible for their own safety when involved in any activity described in this book and that they do so at their own risk.

Substantial discounts are available on bulk quantities of this book when purchased directly from Pride Publications, Inc.

Cover and Photo Pages Design: Philip Ginnodo
Edited by: Joseph J. Ott, Jr.
Maps: K&BW Print Specialties/Bob Webb
Photographs: Bill Ginnodo
Printed in the United States of America by: Fidlar Doubleday, Inc.
The paper used in this publication is acid-free and chlorine-free. It meets the requirements of the American National Standard for Permanence of Paper for Printed Library Materials, ANSI Z39.48-1984.

First Edition/First Printing: 1/07

Library of Congress Cataloging-in-Publication Data

Ginnodo, Bill.
  Seven perfect days in Northern California: a guided driving tour / by Bill and Celia Ginnodo--1st ed.
      p. cm.
 ISBN-13: 978-0-9656587-2-0
 ISBN-10: 0-9656587-2-4
1. California, Northern—Tours. 2. Automobile travel—California, Northern—Guidebooks. I. Ginnodo, Celia, 1936- II. Title
  F867.5.G535 2007
  917.9404'54—dc22
  Library of Congress Control Number: 2006035708

* *

Contents and Highlights

A Special Place

Northern California
> has earthquakes,
> high costs,
> and fog;

But overall,
> it's a beauty,
> an enchantment,
> a joy;

A place to
> explore,
> savor,
> and adore.

It has an ocean,
> mountains,
> gold,
> and wine,

San Francisco,
> Yosemite,
> Lake Tahoe,
> the Golden Gate.

There's much to see,
> learn, and do,
> but take some time
> to smell the roses, too.

We've both experienced Northern California as college students, as employees, as residents, and as travelers. Our three children were born there. We both have relatives living there. Celia was born in Yosemite. So, for us, Northern California is like the Motherland, a special place that we know and love.

We are delighted to be able to share it with you.

— Bill and Celia

Maps and Tour Options

No matter which tour option you choose, your primary map is opposite the title page and called "Seven-Day Tour Route." You'll find 24 more-detailed maps throughout the book. The maps are not to scale. We suggest that you purchase a road map of California to use in conjunction with our maps. It should be available at a bookstore (most of the chain bookstores have them), or you can download the official state map at *www.visitcalifornia.com/state/tourism/tour*. While you're at it, you might want to search that site for other helpful information and download the Official State Visitor's Guide and Travel Planner.

Seven-Day Tour

As shown on the primary map, before the title page, this tour begins in San Francisco, takes a circular route through Northern California and ends a week later in Napa Valley in the Wine Country. Because Oakland is just across the bay from San Francisco, you may fly into and out of either city's airport.

Four-Day Southern Tour

We suggest that you follow the first part of the tour as written—from San Francisco to Monterey to Yosemite and through the Gold Country, finishing in Placerville. Then, take Highway 50 and Interstate 80 back to the San Francisco or Oakland airport to catch an afternoon flight.

Four-Day Northern Tour

For this option, we suggest that you: spend one day in San Francisco; one day in the Wine Country; one day in Old Sacramento and driving to Lake Tahoe; and the fourth day at Lake Tahoe, overnighting in Placerville. Then, as with the Southern Tour, return to the San Francisco or Oakland airport to catch an afternoon flight.

Fourteen-Day Tour, or Create Your Own Tour

We've given you enough alternative attractions in this book that you can easily spend two full days in each location on the tour route. If those suggestions don't suit you, or if you'd rather branch off and do other things, just consult *www.visitcalifornia.com/state/tourism/tour* or the books that we've listed in "Selected Readings."

What You Should Know
About Costs, Reservations, and Yosemite

Our parents taught us, "Forewarned is forearmed."

We don't want to discourage you; it's just that there are several things we think you should know before you begin this trip. If you know them, you'll be able to anticipate and deal with them in advance.

About Costs

California is an expensive place to live and travel. B&B, hotel, and motel costs are all high in California, especially in San Francisco, Monterey-Carmel, and the Wine Country.

In all locations, we have provided a range of accommodations and restaurants to help you find places that meet your budget needs. Since our personal preference is to remain within the aura of those locations, rather than travel elsewhere to save money, we leave it to you to find ways to cut costs. We choose to "wake up where the sun shines on the vine."

We use the following symbols to indicate relative costs for accommodations and restaurants. They are approximate as of the publication of this book.

	Lodging Per Room	Meal Per Person
$	$100 or less	$10 or less
$$	$101-175	$11-20
$$$	$176-300	$21-30
$$$$	$301 and up	$31 and up

About Reservations

We recommend that you make lodging reservations well in advance for Monterey-Carmel, Yosemite (see below), and the Wine Country.

You can save on lodging costs at many establishments by presenting certain membership cards. Therefore, don't forget to ask for your AAA, AARP or other discounts for which you may be eligible!

As for restaurants: During the spring, and summer months, we recommend reservations at least a week in advance for Yosemite's Ahwahnee and Mountain Room Restaurants. Advance reservations are also advised during the summer and fall months for the restaurants listed in the Wine Country chapter (Day Seven).

Yosemite Reservations

Because of its extreme popularity as a tourist destination, Yosemite Valley is, by far, the most difficult place along this tour route to book reservations during the spring, summer, and fall. If you plan to spend a *weekend* night *inside* Yosemite Valley during the summer months, you would be wise to telephone your reservation a full year-and-a-day in advance. Even for weekday reservations during the summer, you may find that your preferred accommodations are not available inside the park several months in advance.

There are lodging choices outside Yosemite—we list many of them in the Day Three chapter—but they also fill rapidly. Our advice is that you reserve as far in advance as possible, and that if you are unable to reserve early, keep in mind that Yosemite Valley reservations can be cancelled seven days in advance of arrival, for a full refund. This means: 1) that you can make your reservation in advance and cancel it without penalty, and 2) that you may be able to get a reservation one week in advance of your arrival if you time your call well.

You May Need to Take an Alternate Route into Yosemite

In April of 2006, there was a huge landslide between Mariposa and El Portal that made Merced Gorge impassable for several months. As of the printing of this book, Highway 140 leading to the west entrance of Yosemite was open, but travelers were experiencing delays while traffic was allowed through alternately, on a one-way basis. *We suggest that you telephone the Yosemite National Park Visitor Center at 209-372-0298 to determine whether Highway 140 is closed and you need to take an alternate route.*

If highway 140 is closed, you can choose to enter Yosemite National Park by either Highway 120 or Highway 41. Highway 41 is the better choice in terms of both distance and time. This will add approximately one hour to your trip. But all is not lost; both highways provide beautiful scenery.

To reach the Park from Mariposa via Highway 41, turn right off Highway 140 onto Highway 49, drive 31 miles east to Oakhurst, then turn left onto Highway 41 and drive northward into the Park.

If you're primarily heading for Yosemite Valley, pass by the Mariposa Grove and enjoy the heavily-wooded landscape on Highway 41/Wawona Road until you get to the Wawona Tunnel. As you emerge from the tunnel, turn *immediately* left into the parking lot and the view will make you forget all about your one-hour delay.

The Day Before Day One

If you're like us, you'll travel to San Francisco in the morning so you can have a bonus afternoon in the area.

What is there to do here that isn't in the seven-day tour? A lot! Following are two options. Also see the list of "Alternative Attractions" at the end of Day One.

Option 1 - Golden Gate Park

We suggest a drive through the park and a visit to two of the following: the Japanese Tea Garden, the Strybing Arboretum, the Conservatory of Flowers, the M.H. de Young Memorial Museum, and the California Academy of Sciences. They are located near each other at the eastern end of the Park and can be reached by driving west from Union Square on Geary Blvd., then south on Stanyan St. All are described at the end of Day One under "Alternative Attractions."

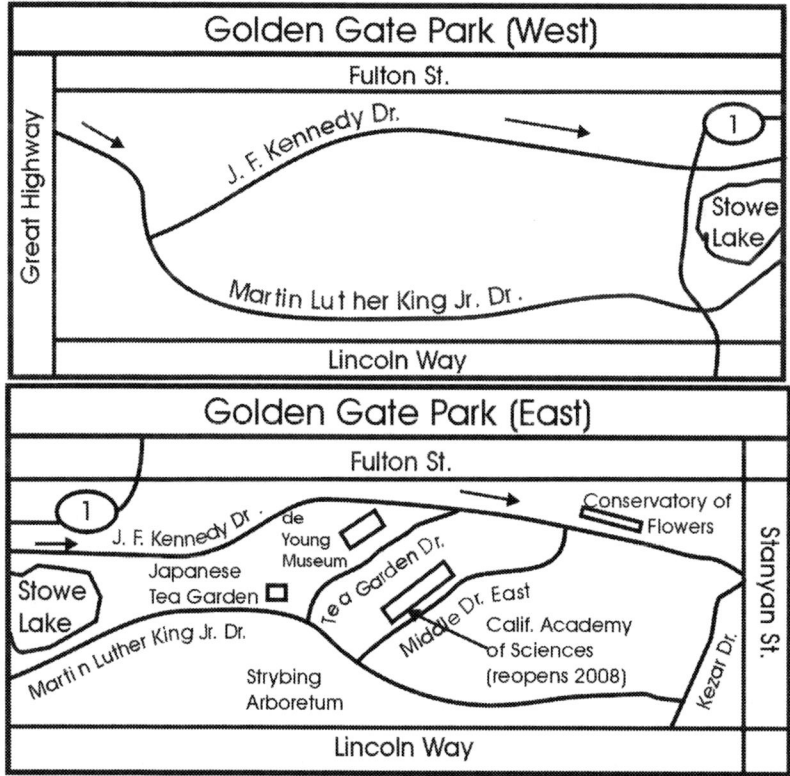

Option 2 - Muir Woods, Hawk Hill, and Sausalito

The Muir Woods National Monument, located 12 miles northwest of the Golden Gate Bridge, contains the Bay Area's only large, intact stand of ancient coast redwood trees—the world's tallest living things. To get there, drive north on U.S. 101, exit at the Mill Valley-Stinson Beach turnoff, and follow twisty-turny Highway 1 to Muir Woods. Walking the one-mile round trip, hard surface, self-guided trail along Redwood Creek, we felt like Lilliputians among the 200 foot-high, 1,000 year-old giants. And there are an interesting variety of birds, ferns and plant life. It's usually cool in these woods, so be sure to have a jacket or sweater handy.

Open every day, including holidays, 8am-8pm during the summer and 8am-5pm during the winter; Muir Woods, Mill Valley 94941; 415-388-2595; *www.nps.gov/muwo.*

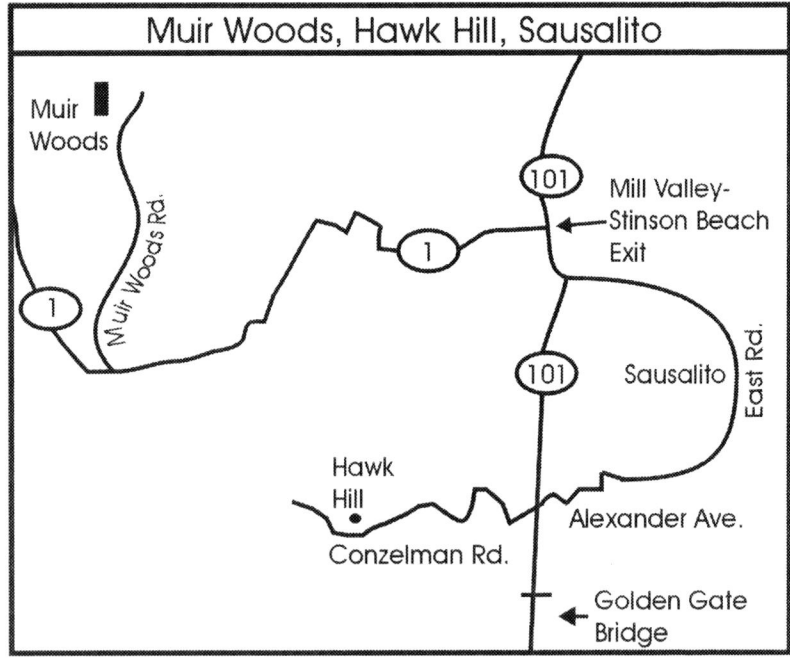

Return to US 101 via Highway 1, take the last exit before the Golden Gate Bridge, and drive up Conzelman Road to Hawk Hill on the Marin Headlands. Here you'll find the area's best view and photo opportunity of San Francisco and the bridge.

Finally, descend Conzelman Road; drive under U.S. 101 and down Alexander Ave. and East Rd. into Sausalito, which is as close to a southern European seacoast hill town as you'll find in the U.S. There you can stroll along the waterfront, browse in the town's many specialty shops, and have dinner at Scoma's. We had our best seafood dinner, ever, at Scoma's, where a reservation is a good idea; 588 Bridgeway Blvd.; 415-332-9551; *www.scomassausallito.com.*

Eat and Sleep

If you follow Option 2, above, and end up in Sausalito, we recommend the Hotel Sausalito, a European-style hotel on the park. It's a bit pricey, but is convenient, very pleasant and provides complimentary morning coffee and pastry. 16 El Portal, Sausalito 94965; 888-442-0700 or 415-332-0700; *www.hotelsausalito.com.*

If you plan to spend tonight and the next night in San Francisco, see our restaurant and lodging recommendations in the coming chapter.

Day One - San Francisco

Many travel guides suggest the 49-mile Drive as the best way to experience San Francisco. If you're going to be here for just one day, we counsel against doing that, because it's too time-consuming and it demands too much stressful city driving If you've already experienced the activities that we've chosen for today, take a look at the alternatives at the end of this chapter and create a day that you'll enjoy.

You've probably heard all the superlatives used to describe the "City by the Bay": "beautiful," "picturesque" "romantic," "enchanting," "charming," "exciting," "alive," "quintessential city" and "everybody's favorite city."

And you probably know why tourists come here—to see the Golden Gate Bridge, Alcatraz, Chinatown, Ghirardelli Square, street performers, and the seals at Fisherman's Wharf. They also come to ride a cable car, to experience the precipitous hills, to taste sourdough bread right where it was created, and to learn why "I Left My Heart in San Francisco" is such a poignant song.

Today, we'll experience these superlatives and tourist clichés. But we'll also see more, do more, learn more, taste more and feel more during this one day than you thought possible...and at a comfortable pace.

This morning, we'll take a scenic drive to see some city highlights, and after that, we'll ride a cable car. This afternoon and into the evening, we'll enjoy the best parts of San Francisco's number one attraction, Fisherman's Wharf.

Be sure to have a sweater, sweatshirt or windbreaker handy—even during the summer, shifting winds and fog can turn the weather chilly in a hurry.

A Bit of Background
Before we start, let's consider some of San Francisco's interesting history and geography, which should help you view it more enjoyably. Historically, the highlights are: establishment of Mission San Francisco de Asis (Mission Dolores) by the Spanish in 1776; establishment of the first settlement here, called Yerba Buena, in 1836; naming of the natural entrance to the bay "the Golden Gate," by explorer John C. Fremont, in 1846; rapid growth of the city to support the California Gold Rush of

1849; and the great earthquake and fire of April 18, 1906 that destroyed 28,000 buildings and killed about 500 people.

Geographically, San Francisco is built on 43 hills and stretches approximately eight miles east-to-west and seven miles north-to-south, encompassing a total area of only 47 square miles. It's often said that if you get tired of climbing, you can always lean against one of the hills. Because the city is surrounded on three sides by water, and the fog rolls in most summer evenings, average daytime temperatures range between 56 and 69 degrees Fahrenheit.

San Francisco has 776,700 residents and draws more than 15 million visitors and business travelers a year. The metropolitan area (called the Bay Area) is the country's fifth largest with 6.8 million residents. This city is a true melting pot of cultures. The leading ethnic groups are Italians, Chinese, Germans, Irish, English, Latin Americans, Japanese, Russians, Filipinos and Koreans.

A Good Map May Come in Handy

We suggest that you obtain the free San Francisco Guide Planning Kit by calling the San Francisco Convention & Visitors Bureau at 415-283-0177 at least a couple of weeks before you leave home. From it, you'll learn of other attractions that are not included in this book. The kit also contains maps, but they are not as detailed as you may desire when you're onsite—especially if you're going to seek out the alternative attractions that we list at the end of this chapter.

The maps that follow are adequate for today's tour route, but we suggest that you purchase a better one from a major bookstore near your home. The best one that we've seen is the San Francisco Street, Recreation and Info Map in Superscale.

Another excellent combination street map and guide (large scale, informally illustrated and footnoted, easy-to-read, color-coded, tear-resistant, waterproof, shows all the sights, many hotels and restaurants, and can be ordered online) is published by MapEasy Guide Maps, PO Box 80, Wainscott, NY 11975, 631-537-6213; *www.mapeasy.com.*

Scenic Driving Tour

Before we start our drive, here are two words of caution: cable cars have the right of way, and, if you park on a hill—even when you put the transmission in "park"—be sure to turn your front wheels so they rest upon the curb and won't roll if the emergency brake doesn't hold.

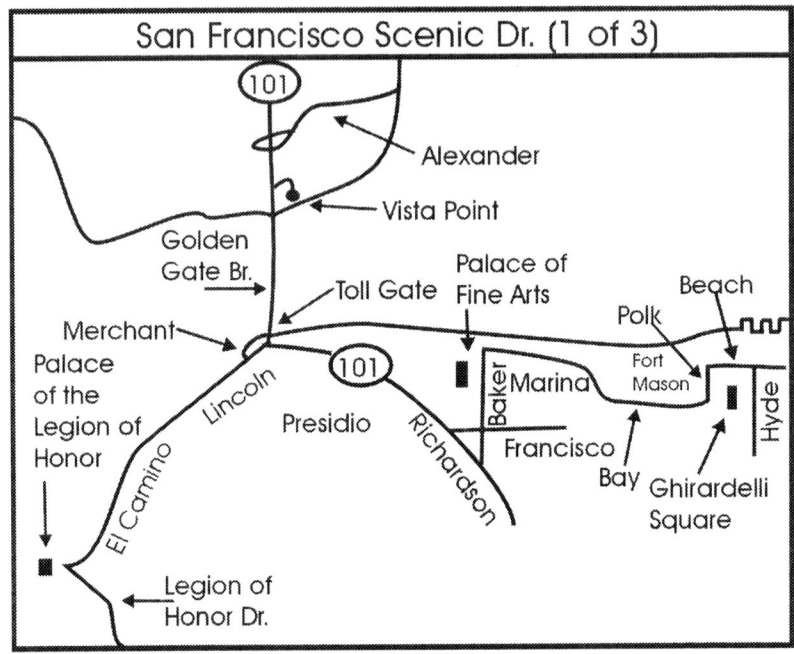

As you can see from our maps, you will be driving across the city from east to west, then from west to east on a different route. On the cable car rides this afternoon, you will experience the city on one route from north to south and on another from south to north. That should give you a good overall perspective of the city.

We're going to begin and end our scenic drive in the Fisherman's Wharf area. That way, your car will be conveniently positioned to get you to your restaurant and accommodations this evening.

Along the way, you'll see signs for the city's 49-mile Scenic Drive, which we think is too long and has too much stressful city driving. Instead, we suggest our tour as more enjoyable: it involves limited driving in the center city, it allows you to see the center city from a cable car, and as a bonus, it allows you to enjoy other activities that we have planned for you.

Our starting point is in front of **Ghirardelli Square** on Beach St., heading west toward the Golden Gate Bridge. This afternoon, we'll spend some time in this complex of charming boutiques and restaurants.

Immediately after Ghirardelli Square, turn left onto Polk St. and then right on Bay St. You'll soon see **Fort Mason Center** on your right. Formerly the western headquarters for the US Army and a WWII troop embarkation point, Fort Mason is now headquarters for the Golden Gate National Recreation Area and the home of several cultural organizations.

Next, you'll drive through the Marina area by turning right on Laguna, left on Beach and right onto Marina Blvd. The Marina area is known for its beautiful homes and exceptional views. *Watch carefully for Baker St., which is the street after Broderick St. If you miss Baker, you'll end up on the Golden Gate Bridge, and we're not ready for that yet.* Turn left (south) onto Baker and you'll find the **Palace of Fine Arts** on your right. We think that the Palace of Fine Arts and the Golden Gate Bridge are the most visually exciting structures in San Francisco—in other words, feasts for the eye.

Here, you'll want to get out of the car, take some photographs and walk through this neo-classical pseudo-Roman ruin. Designed by San Francisco architect, Bernard Maybeck, it was built of wood and plaster as part of the 1915 Panama-Pacific International Exposition and rebuilt in concrete during the 1960's. This is the only structure remaining from the Exposition, which extended from here to Fort Mason.

At the rear of the Palace is the **Exploratorium**, which houses more than 650 hands-on science exhibits; it's great fun for kids and may interest you if you're spending more than a day in San Francisco.

Next, continue south on Baker St. to Francisco St., turn right, and then right again, onto Richardson Ave. Several blocks later, you'll find yourself traveling on U.S. Rte. 101 through the **Presidio's** 1,480 heavily wooded acres toward the Golden Gate Bridge. The Presidio has been of military importance ever since the Spanish established a garrison here in 1776, because of its strategic location at the mouth of San Francisco Bay. The US Army took it over in 1847, and then in 1995 turned it over to the National Park Service.

If you have a keen interest in military history, you may want to tour the Presidio this afternoon, instead of following our tour. Of primary importance is **Fort Point National Historic Site**, which sits directly under the southern base of the Golden Gate Bridge. (You will not be able to see Fort Point from U.S. 101.) Fort Point, with its 126 cannons and 500 soldiers, was modeled after Fort Sumter in North Carolina, and was completed in 1861 to guard the bay during the Civil War. Fort Point's historical museum (415-556-1693) is very worthwhile.

As you approach the **Golden Gate Bridge**, you may be interested to know that: construction of the bridge took 4.5 years, was completed in 1937, and cost $35 million; the bridge is 1.6 miles long, excluding approaches; the center suspension section is 4,200 feet long; the deck sits 220 feet (approximately 22 stories) above the water at low tide; the towers rise another 526 feet (52 stories); its color is "international orange"; and 34 people work full time, year-round, applying 10,000 gallons of paint a year to the bridge.

There is no tollgate northbound on the bridge, because tolls are collected only on the southbound side.

The following two instructions are very important if you want to enjoy a beautiful view of San Francisco and continue to follow our scenic drive without getting off track:

First, be prepared to turn right off U.S. 101 at the Vista Point Exit soon after you leave the bridge. After you do that, you'll find yourself on Vista Point, where you'll want to park and enjoy the view. By the way, the other bridge you'll see from here is the circa-1936 San Francisco-Oakland Bay Bridge. And, of course, that's Oakland at the other end. Berkeley is to the left of Oakland, and, if you look closely, you'll see the pencil-shaped Campanile of our alma mater, the University of California at Berkeley.

The second important instruction is: Reenter U.S. 101 and turn off at the Alexander Ave. Exit. Turn left under 101 and follow the signs to San Francisco to get back to the bridge. As you approach the tollbooth, it's very important that you use the far right-hand lane. Look to the right immediately after exiting the toll booth and turn into the street that you see there. (It looks more like a maintenance road than an exit from a major highway). Continue on that street through the stop sign, and follow Merchant Rd. until it intersects Lincoln Blvd. Turn right on Lincoln.

(If you miss the street immediately after the tollbooth, you will need to follow the Highway 1 signs and exit at Golden Gate Park, picking up the tour from there.)

Then, follow Lincoln south a little over a mile until it turns into El Camino del Mar. Another mile past that, you'll come to the **California Palace of the Legion of Honor**, and the **Holocaust Memorial** which is in the parking circle.

Next, pass in front of the Legion of Honor building and take Legion of Honor Dr. south one-half mile to Geary, where you'll turn right and follow Geary to 39th Ave. Then bear right on Point Lobos Ave. Six-tenths of a mile farther, you'll come to **Cliff House**. You may want to get out of your car here and look 32 miles due west into the Pacific Ocean where you'll see the Farallon Islands. San Francisco's city limits actually extend to, and include, these islands. The Cliff House itself has been the location of a succession of restaurants since 1863, most of which have been leveled by fires. Are you wondering why you don't see very many people on the beach? The reason is that the water is too cold for swimming, year round, and it's unsafe for surfboarding.

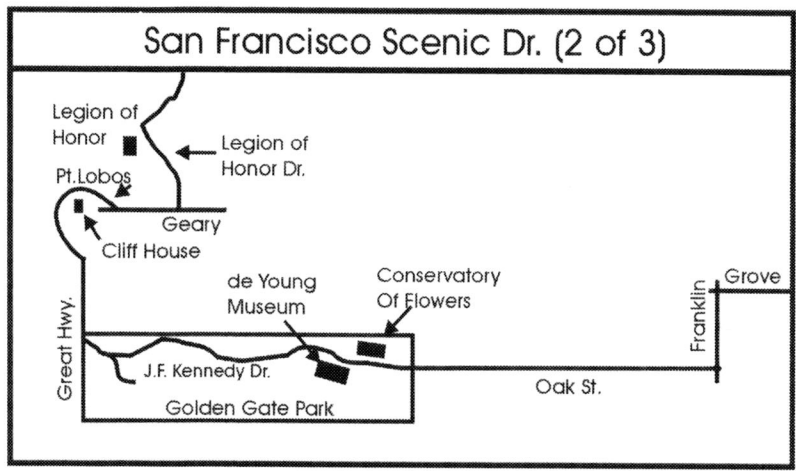

San Francisco Scenic Dr. (2 of 3)

You're now on Great Highway heading south. One-half mile beyond Cliff House, turn left on John F. Kennedy Dr. (just after the traffic light at Fulton St.) and into Golden Gate Park. Follow JFK Drive, which bears left about one-quarter mile into the park, all the way through the park. For more details, see the Golden Gate Park maps in the Day Before Day One chapter.

Golden Gate Park is recognized as one of the most beautiful city parks in the world. It's three miles long and a half-mile wide. Prior to being designed in 1871 by William Hammond Hall and developed by horticulturist John McLaren, its 1,017 acres were windswept and treeless sand dunes.

JFK Dr. will take you by the new **M. H. de Young Museum**, on your right. Nearby are the **Japanese Tea Garden** and the **Strybing Arboretum & Botanical Gardens**. Soon after you pass the de Young Museum, you'll see the **Conservatory of Flowers** on your left. You may have visited several of these attractions yesterday. If not, and if you're spending more time in San Francisco, see "Alternative Attractions," at the end of this chapter, for details.

As you exit Golden Gate Park, the road will feed you onto Oak St. Follow it 1.5 miles to Franklin St., where you'll turn left. Four major streets later, you'll come to Grove St., where you'll turn right and pass between **Symphony Hall** on your right and the **Opera House** on your left. At the next corner, turn left/north onto Van Ness and drive past **City Hall** on your right. Nine major streets past City Hall turn right/east onto Bush St. Another ten major streets and you'll arrive at the green-tiled Chinatown Gate on Grant Ave. Turn left on Grant and enter Chinatown.

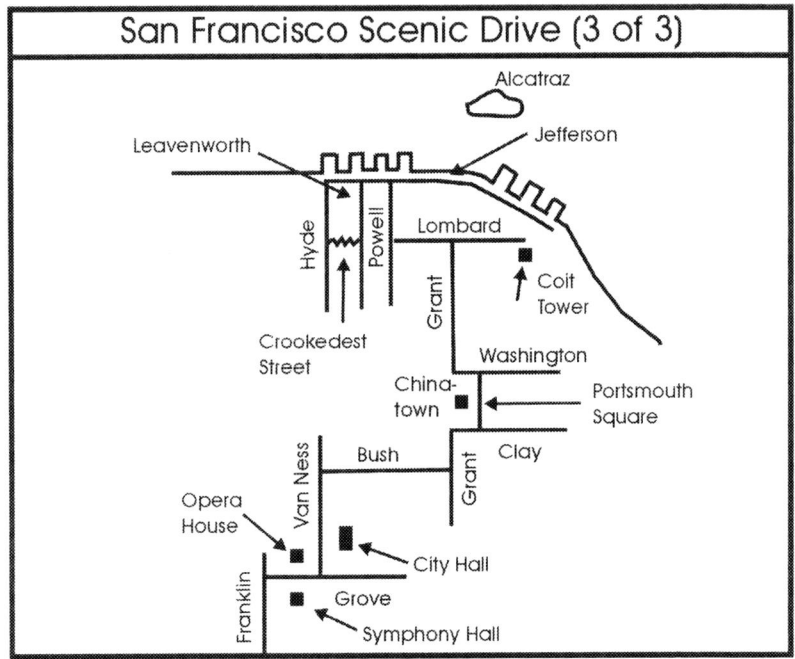

Chinatown is an enclave of 18 square blocks that has the largest concentration of Chinese outside Asia (about 13,000 people). Many of the people you see here are recent immigrants, because Chinatown is a kind of revolving door. Newcomers continually take the place of those who have become acclimated to America and move on to other parts of the city or country. Look at the storefronts closely to see if you can determine what kinds of businesses serve the local residents and tourists.

Two major streets north of Bush St., you'll come to Clay St. Turn right and travel one block to Kearney St., then turn left. On your left is Portsmouth Square.

Portsmouth Square has four distinctions: 1) before landfill changed the landscape, it was on the waterfront; 2) originally, it was the plaza of the Mexican settlement of Yerba Buena; 3) it's the site where the American flag was first raised on San Francisco in July, 1846; and, 4) today, it's an important gathering place for the Chinese community.

At the end of the block, turn left on Washington St., and then right on Grant St. Nine major streets north on Grant, you'll come to Lombard St. Turn right on Lombard and drive two streets to Telegraph Hill Blvd. Then, drive up the hill to **Coit Tower.**

You'll then be on top of **Telegraph Hill** looking at a beautiful panorama of San Francisco and the bay. To the north you'll see **Alcatraz Island** and **Fisherman's Wharf.** To the south is the **Ferry Building** and the **Transamerica Pyramid**, the city's tallest building at 853 feet. The 210-foot Coit Tower was built in 1933, from a bequest by Lillie Hitchcock Coit, to honor the city's firefighters. Works Progress Administration murals can be viewed on the first floor of the tower. There is an elevator to the top.

Now drive back down to Lombard St., then turn left and drive three streets to Powell where you'll turn right. Six streets down Powell you'll come to Jefferson, where you'll turn left and drive five streets to Hyde. Jefferson Street is the heart of **Fisherman's Wharf**.

From Jefferson, you'll get a closer view of Alcatraz Island out in the bay. Although benign-looking from a distance, this former fort, military prison and federal maximum-security penitentiary (from 1934 to 1963) has often been called a "hell hole." Famous inmates included Al Capone, "Machine Gun" Kelley, Mickey Cohen and Robert "Birdman of Alcatraz" Stroud. Tours of "The Rock" leave from Pier 33 at the east end of Bay Street. If you're staying longer and are interested, see "Alternate Attractions" at the end of this chapter.

When we return to Fisherman's Wharf after the cable car ride, we'll walk the water side of Jefferson, enjoying the street performers, seafood stalls and moored fishing boats. Just before you turn left onto Hyde St., look to the right and you'll see the historic ships that we'll board this afternoon.

After turning onto Hyde, you'll see the cable car turnaround-embarkation point on your right just before Beach St. That is where you'll catch the cable car after seeing the Crookedest Street.

Continue past Beach, uphill five streets, to Lombard, and then turn left down the hill.

The Crookedest Street in the World

This block of Lombard Street on Russian Hill is known as "The Crookedest Street in the World." The hill is so steep that eight curves were added in the 1920's so horse-drawn carriages could negotiate it. A resident by the name of Peter Bercut added the Hydrangeas in the 1950's. Today, it's great fun to drive or walk down, and beautiful to photograph from the bottom, especially in the morning when the sun is fully on it. So when you reach the end of the block, if you have your camera ready and the opportunity to street-park....

At the bottom of the Crookedest Street, turn left onto Leavenworth, then drive five streets back to Beach St. and turn left.

On the left, in the middle of the next block (between Leavenworth and Hyde) you'll find a parking garage where we suggest you leave your car until this evening. (An alternative is the Ghirardelli Square underground parking garage that is two blocks farther west; enter on Larkin St.)

Now, walk one-half block west to the cable car turnaround-embarkation point.

Cable Car Ride

It was Andrew Hallidie who, having witnessed the accident of an overloaded horse-drawn streetcar on Nob Hill, conceived the mechanism under the cable car that grips and releases the constantly moving steel cable. This enables the car to move forward, climb hills, and descend hills safely.

Beginning in 1873, cable cars became the primary means of public transportation in San Francisco. By 1906, the system had eight lines with 115 miles of track and 600 cable cars. Today only three lines, 10.5 miles of track and 30 cars survive, and the city's cable car system is a National Historic Landmark. The system carries some 13 million passengers a year, more than half of whom are local residents.

You should be able to get on a Powell-Hyde cable car going toward Union Square at this time of day. For the best views, we suggest that you sit on the left outside seats. We also suggest that you put away this book and simply enjoy the sights and sounds of this wonderful, 9-1/2 mph, 15- to 20-minute experience. If you're seated, be sure to have your camera ready for some great views, especially on your left at the top of Nob Hill at the intersection of California and Powell. (See the cable car photograph at the front of this book for a view from the top of The Crookedest Street in the World, looking toward Coit Tower.)

Things may get a little more difficult on the return trip, because there's likely to be a waiting line at the Hallidie Plaza turntable. You'll want to return via the Powell-Mason Line, so you can enjoy different scenery, and to position yourself for our next activity. You'll end up at the turntable at Taylor and Bay Streets. Walk three blocks toward the bay to Jefferson, turn right and walk three blocks to Pier 39. *Instead of waiting in Hallidie Plaza, you may want to hail a cab on Market St. and ask the driver to take you to Pier 39 at Fisherman's Wharf.* There are some wonderful attractions at Fisherman's Wharf, and we're going to visit them this afternoon. However, a large number of tacky establishments have sprung up to exploit the many tourists who flock here. You may have different tastes than we do, but we choose to put blinders on, quickly pass them by, and head toward the attractions that are truly worthwhile.

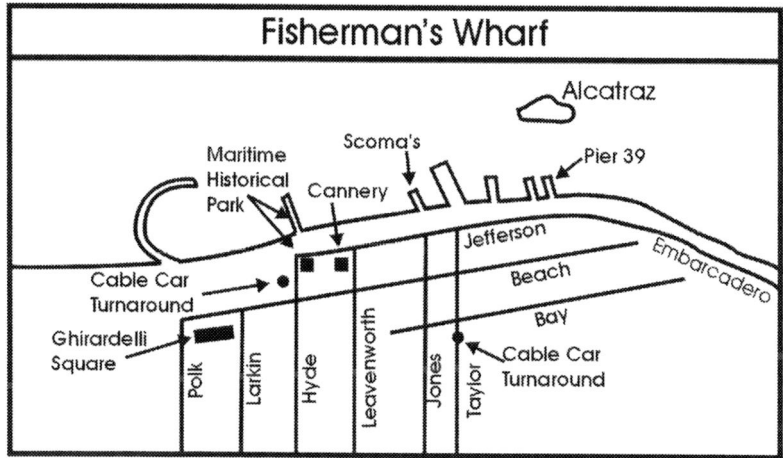

The Seals at Pier 39

Not one of our favorite attractions because we find it too commercialized and lacking in typical San Francisco charm, Pier 39 is nevertheless one of the city's most-visited sites. Good for kids, it features an aquarium, arcade rides, scenic bay cruises, restaurants, and more than 100 specialty shops. The end of the pier is a good vantage point for taking photographs of Alcatraz, especially if you have a telephoto lens. But Pier 39's biggest attraction is also its noisiest.

If you don't have children with you, we suggest you walk straight through the center of the pier, turn left, then left again to the sea lion overlook. Our first time here, we spent about 45 minutes watching, listening and truly enjoying this unusual sight. Altogether, we counted 40 rafts that each averaged about 25 sea lions and harbor seals. That's about 1,000 of the noisy and amusing creatures in one location. Celia thought they were "hilarious." What's the difference between a sea lion and a harbor seal? Adult sea lions are dark brown or black, have ears, are often seven or eight feet in length, and can weigh up to 800 pounds. Harbor seals are usually light gray or brown and are spotted, do not have ears, are five to six feet long, and weigh about 200 pounds. About 1990, boats occupied this entire area. Then the sea lions and seals began to winter here. The people in charge of tourism realized they had a bonanza, so the boats were moved out and the animals moved in. For a good picture of the overall scene, head for Pier 41 across the way (the vantage point of the photograph at the front of this book).

It's Lunch Time!

Now, walk west on Jefferson to its intersection with Taylor Street. (Along the way, you'll probably see some of the city's licensed street performers.) Here you'll find some fine-smelling, picturesque, outdoor seafood stalls. Sauntering by them should whet your appetite. If you're on a tight budget, you may choose to stay right here and munch on Dungeness crab-in-a-cup and sourdough bread.

Instead, we recommend Scoma's restaurant as a far better, and better tasting, experience. As we do throughout this book, we list a fairly wide choice of restaurants for dinner, but we get rather specific for lunch. Today, we suggest that you continue west one block to the junction of Jefferson and Jones Streets. Then walk out onto the pier, which is the home of the fishing fleet that supplies the Wharf's seafood restaurants. When you see the orange and white Scoma's sign on your left, you'll know you're there. Don't be put off by the restaurant's unpretentious appearance; it's what's inside that counts.

Scoma's has been our favorite San Francisco lunch spot for many years, and it is a favorite of many San Franciscans, too. For us, the reason is the restaurant's large Crab Louis salad, which is scrumptious. Forget what it costs and dig into that huge mound of Dungeness crab that's covered with a very tasty Thousand Island dressing. (It makes our mouths water just to think about it!) With Scoma's sourdough bread, this is a truly sensational meal. If you can't abide crab or even seafood, the restaurant also has a wide selection of salads, pasta and meat dishes to choose from. (415-771-4383; *www.scomas.com*)

After lunch, continue walking west on Jefferson. You'll see **The Cannery** on your left. It's a three-story shopping center built inside the circa-1909 Del Monte peach-canning factory. We'll pass up The Cannery in preference to Ghirardelli Square, which we'll visit in a little while. But if The Cannery appeals to you more than our next activity does, go for it and enjoy! (2801 Leavenworth St., 415-771-3112, *www.thecannery.com*)

Historic Ships

When you reach Hyde St., turn right and walk out onto the Hyde Street Pier. There you'll enter the **San Francisco Maritime National Historical Park** (that's a mouthful, isn't it?).

Nowhere else in the United States is there a collection of five ships that have been designated as a National Historic Landmark. You can board and explore three of them!

The star of the show is the *Balclutha*, a 256-foot long, three-masted, square-rigged, steel-hulled sailing ship that was built in 1886 in Glasgow, Scotland. It has seen a lot of open ocean, because it's primary task was to carry California wheat to Europe and to return with whiskey and coal. In doing so, it rounded the treacherous southern tip of South America (Cape Horn) 17 times.

Here's your opportunity for a unique experience. Try to imagine how challenging and difficult life was for the sailors who occupied a cramped bunk area while under sail for months at a time, or as they climbed high in the ship's rigging during good weather or bad. Stand at the helm and imagine guiding the ship around the Cape during a violent storm. Check out the captain's cabin and the below-deck maritime museum. Join an interpretive presentation by a Park ranger. In other words, this may be your once-in-a-lifetime opportunity to get a genuine *feel* for what it was like to sail the ocean in the 1800's.

On a personal note, your guide, Bill, in more youthful days spent a couple of months employed as a fisherman on a tuna clipper off South America. Every visit here brings back memories of: being on the high seas for many days with no land in sight; horizon-to-horizon "red skies in the morning" followed by two days in a hurricane; millions of seabirds overhead off Peru diving for anchovies; the back-breaking labor of pulling tuna on board with a cane fishing pole, and the teamwork required with other fishermen.

Next, board the *C.A. Thayer,* a 156-foot long, three-masted schooner built in 1895. One of two surviving schooners from a fleet of 900, she was the last commercial sailing vessel on the West Coast. *Thayer* carried lumber between Puget Sound and various California ports, as well as fishermen and small boats to Alaska, returning with salmon. She also served as a cod fishing boat in the Bering Sea.

Finally, climb aboard the *Eureka*, a 299-foot side-wheel ferry built in 1890 in Tiburon, just across the bay. Her original name, *Ukiah*, was changed to *Eureka* when refitted in 1922 to carry automobiles and passengers instead of trains. *Eureka* was the world's largest passenger ferry, capable of carrying 2,300 passengers and 120 automobiles per trip. Be sure to check out the lower deck where you'll find a display of classic autos and trucks.

The other two national historic landmark ships, which you'll have to observe from the pier, are the *Alma*, a 59-foot, flat-bottomed scow schooner built in San Francisco in 1891, and the *Hercules*, a 139-foot steam-powered tugboat built in Camden, New Jersey in 1907. Not in the landmark category, but interesting nevertheless, is the *Eppleton Hall*, a 100-foot steam-powered steel tugboat that was built in South Shields, England in 1914.

The Historical Park's Visitor Center is also worth a visit. You'll find it as you leave the Hyde St. Pier at the corner of Jefferson and Hyde. Its displays tell interesting stories of voyage and discovery. 415-447-5000; *www.nps.gov/safr*.

If you're really into ships, the **Maritime Museum** is two blocks west on Beach St., and there are two other ships worthy of your attention on Pier 45 at the foot of Taylor St.: the **USS Pampanito** submarine and the **S.S. Jeremiah O'Brien** liberty ship. They are described at the end of this chapter, under "Alternative Attractions."

Ghirardelli Square

Next, walk up Hyde St., past the cable car turnaround to Beach St., then a block west to Ghirardelli Square. As you do, you'll pass a favorite of both the locals and tourists, the Buena Vista Cafe, at 2765 Hyde (415-474-5044). There's a reason the Buena Vista Cafe is always crowded: it's the home (and principal dispenser in the world) of the original Irish coffee, a blend of Irish whiskey, black coffee, sugar, and heavy cream.

Ghirardelli Square (415-775-5500; *www.ghirardellisq.com*) has the distinction of being the first manufacturing facility in the U.S. to be converted to a shopping and restaurant complex. The oldest of the red brick buildings, circa 1864 and originally a woolen mill, became the Ghirardelli Chocolate Factory. It operated as such from 1893 to 1962 when the company transferred its operations to a new factory across the bay in San Leandro. The square was transformed to its current use by 1964.

Containing more than 40 businesses, Ghirardelli Square has an appeal about it that other similar complexes can't quite match. From the entrance fountain and view of the bay to the inviting plaza, free entertainment, restaurants, quality shops, international merchandise, and foods, this is a class operation.

Be sure to visit the Ghirardelli Chocolate Manufactory to observe chocolate being made by the original equipment, as well as to view the store's extensive selection of chocolates. You can also get free samples at the door of the less-crowded Ghirardelli Soda Fountain and Chocolate Shop.

If you haven't spoiled your appetite by eating too much chocolate, Ghirardelli Square is a good place to have your evening meal. Two notable restaurants are located right here: The Mandarin and McCormick and Kuleto's. They are included in the listing immediately below.

It's Dinnertime!
San Francisco is filled with excellent restaurants of every imaginable cuisine. Your innkeeper or concierge should be able to zero-in on a restaurant or two that will satisfy your taste buds or be near your accommodations. Here are some in or near Fisherman's Wharf that we have especially enjoyed or that come well recommended by others:

* **Fog City Diner**, California cuisine, 1300 Battery St. (east of Coit Tower), San Francisco 94111, 415-982-2000, *www. fogcitydiner.com*, $$.
* **Il Fornaio**, Italian/Tuscan, 1265 Battery St. (east of Coit Tower), San Francisco 94111, 415-986-0100, *www. ilfornaio.com*, $$-$$$.
* **Julius' Castle**, American and European cuisine, 1541 Montgomery St. (east of Coit Tower), San Francisco 94133, 415-392-2222, *www. juliuscastle.com*, $$$-$$$$.
* **L'Osteria Del Forno**, Italian cuisine, 519 Columbus Ave. (between Green and Union), San Francisco 94133, 415-982-1124, *www.losteriadelforno.com*, $$.
* **The Mandarin**, northern Chinese cuisine, upscale ambiance, 900 North Point St. (in Ghirardelli Square), San Francisco 94109, 415-673-8812, *www.themandarin.com*, $$.
* **McCormick and Kuleto's**, seafood menu, 900 North Point St. (in Ghirardelli Square), San Francisco 94109, 415-929-1730, *www. mccormickandkuletos.com*, $$.
* **Rico's**, Mexican cuisine, 943 Columbus Ave., (between Taylor and Lombard), San Francisco, 415- 928-5404, *www.ricosinc. com*, $$.

- **Scoma's** (a favorite of ours), seafood menu, Al Scoma Way (Pier 47), San Francisco 94133, 800-644-5852, 415-771-4383, *www.scomas.com*, $$$.

About San Francisco Accommodations

Since this day's tour both begins and ends in Fisherman's Wharf, we thought that you would find it most convenient to spend your nights there as well. And by choosing lodging in that area, you would have the added benefit of convenient and assured parking (night and day; though often for a fee).

If you choose to go farther away, the AAA and Mobile travel guides are excellent resources for hotels and motels.

If you prefer the bed and breakfast/inn route, we've listed some that are reasonably close to Fisherman's Wharf. For other B&Bs, we suggest that you access these online resources: *www.cabbi.com*, *www.bbonline. com*, *www.innsite.com,* and *www.bedandbreakfast.com.*

Ginnodo-recommended B&Bs/Inns

- **The Archbishop's Mansion**, 1000 Fulton St., San Francisco 94117, 800-543-5820, 415-563-7872, fax 415-885-3193, *www. jdvhospitality.com/hotels/hotel/2*, $$$-$$$$.
- **Chateau Tivoli Bed & Breakfast**, 1057 Steiner St., San Francisco 94115, 800-228-1647, 415-776-5462, fax 415-776-0505, *www.chateautivoli.com*, $$-$$$.
- **Edward II Inn & Suites**, 3155 Scott St. San Francisco 94123, 800-473-2846, 415-922-3000, 415-931-5784, *www.edwardii. com*, $-$$$.
- **Golden Gate Hotel**, 775 Bush St., San Francisco 94108, 800-835-1118, 415-392-3702, fax 415-392-6202, *www.goldengate hotel.com*, $-$$.
- **Inn San Francisco**, 943 S. Van Ness, San Francisco 94110, 800-359-0913, 415-641-0188, fax 415-641-1701, *www.innsf. com*, $$-$$$.
- **Queen Anne Hotel**, 1590 Sutter St., San Francisco 94109, 800-227-3970, 415-441-2828, fax 415-775-5212, *www.queenanne. com,* $$-$$$.
- **Union Street Inn**, 229 Union St., San Francisco 94123, 415-346-0424, fax 415-922-8046, *www.unionstreetinn.com*, $$-$$$.
- **Washington Square Inn**, 1660 Stockton St., San Francisco 94133, 800-388-0220, 415-981-4220, fax 415-397-7242, *www. wsisf.com*, $$-$$$.

AAA- or Mobil-recommended Motels/Hotels

- **Argonaut Hotel**, 495 Jefferson St., San Francisco 94109, 866-415-0704, 415-563-0800, fax 415-563-2800, *www.argonaut hotel.com*, $$-$$$.
- **Buena Vista Motor Inn**, 1599 Lombard St., San Francisco 94123, 800-835-4980, 415-923-9600, fax 415-441-4775, *www. buenavistamotorinn.com*, $$.
- **Columbus Motor Inn**, 1075 Columbus Ave., San Francisco 94133, 415-885-1492, fax 415-928-2174, *www.columbusmotor inn.com*, $-$$.
- **Comfort Inn By the Bay**, 2775 Van Ness Ave., San Francisco 94109, 415-928-5000, fax 415-441-3990, *www.choicehotels. com*, $$-$$$.
- **Holiday Inn Fisherman's Wharf**, 1300 Columbus Ave., San Francisco 94133, 800-288-4595, 415-771-9000, fax 415-771-7006, *www.ichotelsgroup.com*, $$$.
- **Marina Inn**, 3110 Octavia St., San Francisco 94123, 800-274-1420, 415-928-1000, fax 415-928-5909, *www.marinainn.com*, $$.
- **San Francisco Marriott Fisherman's Wharf**, 1250 Columbus Ave., San Francisco 94133, 800-228-9290, 415-775-7555, fax 415-474-2099, *www.marriott.com*, $$$.
- **Sheraton Fisherman's Wharf**, 2500 Mason St., San Francisco 94133, 800-325-3535, 415-362-5500, fax 415-956-5275, *www. sheratonatthewharf.com*, $$-$$$.
- **Tuscan Inn**, 425 North Point St., San Francisco 94133, 800-648-4626, 415-561-1100, fax 415-561-1199, *www.tuscaninn. com*, $$.

Woodall's-recommended Campgrounds

- **Candlestick RV Park** San Francisco; from 3 Com Park exit on Hwy 101, drive around the stadium to Gate 4; 800-888-2267, fax 415-822-7638, *www.sanfranciscorvpark.com*.
- **San Francisco RV Resort**, Pacifica; from jct. of Hwy 1 & Interstate 280, drive 2-1/2 mi. S on Hwy 1to Manor/Palmetto Dr. exit, then 3 blocks S on Palmetto Ave.; 800-822-1250, *www.sanfranciscorvresort.com*.
- **Trailer Villa**, Redwood City; leave US 101 at Seaport Blvd., turn right on E. Bayshore Rd., 1-1/4 mi. to Trailer Villa; 800-366-7880, 650-366-7880.

- **Golden Gate Trailer Court**, San Rafael; from northbound US 101 exit at Lucky Dr., then drive 1 block S on E Frontage Rd.; 415-924-0683.

*****

ALTERNATIVE ATTRACTIONS

** *In the Fisherman's Wharf Area* **

Alcatraz Island - Operational as a federal penitentiary from 1934 to 1963, Alcatraz opened to visitors in 1973 and is now one of San Francisco's most popular tourist attractions. The visit includes a self-guided audiotape tour of the cell house featuring the voices of former guards and inmates. Ranger-led tours are available. Alcatraz Cruises tours leave only from Pier 33 at the east end of Bay Street, Fisherman's Wharf.

Contact 415-561-4900 or *www.nps.gov/goga/alcatraz* for National Park Service information. Contact 415-981-7625 or *www.alcatraz cruises.com* for Alcatraz Cruises reservations. Tickets can be purchased in person at the Hornblower Alcatraz Landing ticket office at Pier 33. Departure times are approximately every 1/2-hour from 9:30am to 4:15pm. Total tour time is about 2-1/2 hours.

Maritime Museum - Situated in **Aquatic Park**, across the street from Ghirardelli Square, this museum features ship models, bowsprits and other large ship parts, navigational instruments, artwork, historic photos, and other nautical artifacts. Part of the San Francisco Maritime National Historic Park. 900 Beach St.; open daily 10am-5pm; 415-561-7100; *www.nps.gov/safr*.

S.S. Jeremiah O'Brien Liberty Ship - At 441 feet in length, this is the last of the 957 WWII ships that transported troops and wartime supplies to and from the Pacific Theater.

Berthed at Pier 45 (foot of Taylor St.); open daily 9am-4pm; 415-544-0100; *www.ssjeremiahobrien.com*.

USS Pampanito Submarine - This 311-ft long sub fought many battles in the Pacific during WWII, sinking six enemy ships. Learn what life was like inside a wartime submarine via an audio taped tour.

Berthed at Pier 45 (foot of Taylor St.); open from 9am-8pm June through October and 9am-6pm November through May; 415-775-1943; *www.maritime.org.*

** *In Golden Gate Park* **

California Academy of Sciences - The academy is in a temporary location until its new building in Golden Gate Park is completed in late 2008. Normally, this is three museums in one: The **Steinhart Aquarium** displays 16,000 marine specimens in 190 tanks and features a fish roundabout, a coral reef and a frozen great white shark. The **Natural History Museum** features excellent animal dioramas. The **Morrison Planetarium** features a laser light show, but is closed until the new building is complete in late 2008.

875 Howard Street; open every day of the year 10am-5pm; 415-321-8000; *www.calacademy.org.*

Conservatory of Flowers - Housed in a replica of the conservatory in Kew Gardens, England, this large greenhouse contains palms, philodendrons, orchids, ferns, hibiscuses and other rare plants.

JFK Drive; open Thursday-Sunday, 9am-4:30pm; 415-666-7001; *www.conservatoryofflowers.org.*

Japanese Tea Garden – Five acres of Japanese landscaping, featuring a dwarf tree forest, a giant bronze Buddha cast in Japan in 1790, colorful pagodas, the moon bridge, pretty waterfalls, a temple, lanterns, cherry blossoms peaking about the first week of April, and a teahouse staffed by Japanese women.

Tea Garden Drive; open daily 8:30am-5:30pm; 415-752-4227; *www.frp.org/Japanese_tea_garden.*

M.H. de Young Memorial Museum - A collection of 1,000 American paintings, American sculpture and decorative art, African art, Oceanic art, art of the Americas, textiles, and contemporary crafts.

Hagiwara Tea Garden Drive; open Tuesday-Sunday 9:30am-5pm, Friday until 8:45pm; 415-863-3330; *www.thinker.org/deyoung.*

Strybing Arboretum & Botanical Gardens - Sixty acres of carefully labeled plant varieties and species from around the world, arranged according to geographical origin.

Ninth Avenue at Lincoln Way; open 365 days from 8am-4:30pm weekdays and 10am-5pm on weekends and holidays; 415-661-1316; *www.sfbotanicalgarden.org*.

** Elsewhere in San Francisco **

Asian Art Museum - Relocated in 2003 from Golden Gate Park to the former library building in Civic Center, this museum holds the largest collection of Asian art in the country, some 13,000 items spanning 60 centuries of history throughout Asia.

200 Larkin St.; open Tuesday through Sunday 10am-5pm and Thursday until 9pm; 415-581-3500; *www.asianart.org*.

Cable Car Museum - This has been the central powerhouse of the cable car system since 1873. It also is a museum containing original cable cars, scale models and photographs. Observe the winding gear and 57,300 feet of steel cable in action.

1201 Mason St. at Washington St.; open 10am-5pm October 1-March 31 and 10-6 April 1-September 30; 415-474-1887; *www.cablecar museum.org*.

California Palace of the Legion of Honor - Patterned after the Palais de la Legion d'Honneur in Paris, this museum houses ancient art from 2500 BC, tapestries, and paintings and sculpture by artists such as Degas, El Greco, Monet, Picasso, Rembrandt, Rodin, Rubens, and Seurat. One of five existing bronze-cast statues of Rodin's *The Thinker* sits at the entrance to the museum. Also see the Holocaust Memorial in the parking circle in front of the museum.

34th Ave. and Clement St. in Lincoln Park; open 9:30am-5pm Tuesday through Sunday and 9:30am-8:45pm the first Saturday of the month; 415-750-3600; *www.legionofhonor.org*.

Exploratorium - At the back of the Palace of Fine arts, this museum of science, technology and human perception features more than 650 exhibits that can be activated and manipulated by kids and adults alike.

3601 Lyon St.; open Tuesday through Sunday from 10am-5pm; 415-397-5673; *www.exploratorium.edu*.

Mission Dolores - Sixth in the chain of missions established in 1776 by Father Junipero Serra and his Franciscans, this oldest complex in the city comprises a church (1782), paintings, period artifacts, and a cemetery with 5,000 Indians stacked in layers. 3321 16th St.; open daily 8am to noon and 1pm-4pm; 415-621-2294; *www.missiondolores.citysearch.com.*

San Francisco Museum of Modern Art - Designed by Swiss architect Mario Botta and completed in 1995, the building is itself a work of art. The museum contains an extensive collection of 20th-century paintings, sculpture and photographs, an architecture and design collection, a media arts collection, and has frequent exhibits.

151 Third St.; open daily except Wednesday and major holidays 11am-5:45pm, and Thursday 11am-8:45pm; 415-357-4000; *www.sfmoma.org.*

** *North of San Francisco* **

Muir Woods and Sausalito are both close to San Francisco. Allow a full day for the Point Reyes National Seashore, and two days for the Highway 1 drive to Mendocino. The best travel times are May to early June, and September to late October. Expect morning fog during the summer. Bring warm clothing at all times of the year. Accommodations may be scarce, so arrange lodging in advance.

Muir Woods and Sausalito - See the prior chapter, "The Day Before Day One," for a description and directions on how to get there.

Point Reyes National Seashore

Located 25 miles north of San Francisco, Point Reyes is the largest peninsula on the northern California coast and a good place to "get away from it all." Explorer Sir Francis Drake is said to have landed here in 1579. The park is best known today for its 100-plus miles of wilderness hiking trails, wonderful ocean panoramas, and the lighthouse which clings to the end of the Point, 308 steps down from the lighthouse station itself. Also worth seeing are the excellent exhibits in the Bear Valley Visitor Center, which is located in the park one mile from the town of Olema, and the nearby Morgan Horse Farm, Coast Miwok Indian Village, and Earthquake Trail, where you can clearly see how the earth has shifted along the San Andreas fault line. (Point Reyes is still moving northwest at two inches a year.) We saw quite a few deer, many species of birds, and a single tree with thousands of holes bored by woodpeckers. Migrating gray whales can be seen from Point Reyes between December and February, and between March and May.

The Bear Valley Visitor Center is open Monday-Friday 9am-5pm and weekends and holidays 8am-5pm (closed December 25); 415-464-5100; *www.nps.gov/pore*. The Lighthouse Visitor Center is open Thursday-Monday 10am-4:30pm; 415-669-1534. The Morgan Horse Ranch is open daily 9am-4:30pm; 415-646-5169.

Highway 1 Drive and Mendocino

The best and most famous coastal drive in California is the 26-miles of Highway 1 between Carmel and the village of Big Sur. In our opinion, the next best is the 77 miles between Jenner and Mendocino. Much of it is high above the ocean, affording dramatic and gorgeous views of the coastline and ocean. You'll travel through interesting small coastal towns and past headlands that jut out into the ocean and in springtime are covered with wildflowers. The isolation and beauty of this stretch of coast make it feel like another world.

Fort Ross State Historic Park, about 20 miles north of Jenner, is a very worthwhile stop. This was the southernmost settlement of Russians who came here in 1812 and trapped sea otters along the coast until 1841. The visitor center provides excellent information and the fort is interesting to tour.

Also of interest are the many beaches along this part of the coast. Our favorites are Walk On Beach and Bowling Ball Beach near Sea Ranch.

There are several very good restaurants in and near Gualala, as well as a regional park that provides good hiking and nature study.

Elk and Mendocino have good bed-and-breakfasts. A visit to photogenic **Point Arena Lighthouse**, just south of Manchester, is also worthwhile. (See the photograph at the front of this book.)

Mendocino is an out-of-the-way fitting terminus to this drive. Its beautiful cliff-top coastal setting, picturesque New England-style houses, interesting shops, and Artists Co-op and Art Center make this a very enjoyable destination. Mendocino has been the setting for TV's *Murder She Wrote* and several movies, and is well known as an artist's colony. The entire town is on the National Register of Historic Places.

The quick way back to the "real world" is via U.S. 101 South.

Day Two - **Monterey and Carmel**

This is an "if" (not "iffy) day: If you're touring during the summer, you're likely to encounter fog along the coast until mid morning. If the fog is dense, you may be better off taking the inland freeway route to Monterey and Carmel. If there is no fog, you can follow the tour as presented. And if you get an early enough start, you should be able to complete today's itinerary.

Today we'll take the coast drive down to Monterey and Carmel, where we'll enjoy Old Monterey, Cannery Row, the Monterey Bay Aquarium, the 17-Mile Drive, and Carmel Mission. After dinner, we'll cruise what may be the most art galleries in one place in the U. S.

If there's dense fog when you get ready to leave San Francisco, we recommend that you take a more inland route: Interstate 280 to US 101, 101 to California 156, and 156 to California 1 which goes into Monterey. (See the following map for this alternate route as well as the coast route that we hope you'll be able to take.) Fog is common to this area in the summer months and both obscures the views from the coastal road and presents an element of driving risk that you may want to avoid.

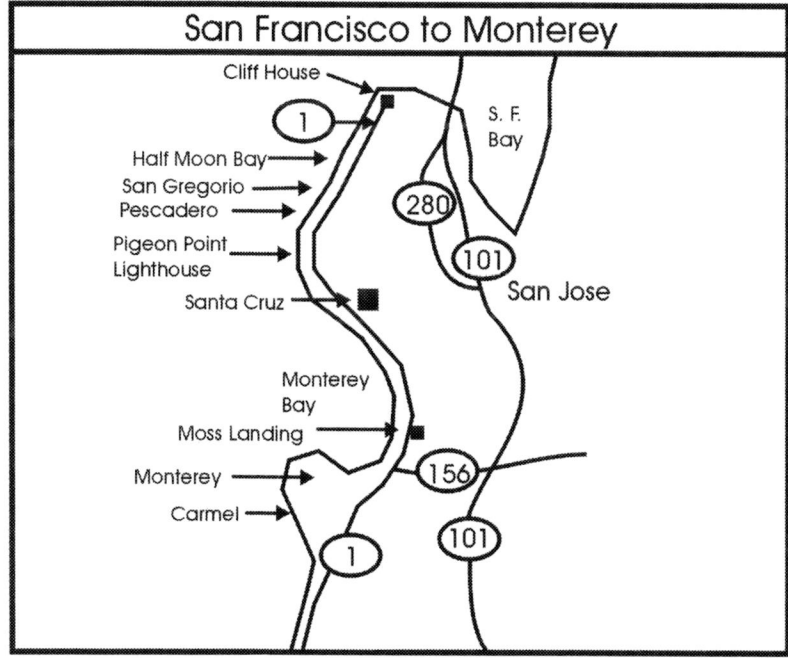

A Drive Down the Coast

We're now going to experience 130 miles of California's beautiful 840-mile Pacific coastline. The *piece de resistance* is the Monterey Peninsula's 17-Mile Drive. There, we'll enjoy the Drive's spectacular scenery and take a walk on the beach.

We'll start high on a bluff at Cliff House in San Francisco and end up viewing the underwater environment of Monterey Bay—a metaphorical two and one-half hour gradual slide into the sea.

To get to Cliff House in San Francisco, drive west on Geary and Point Lobos Streets (see the map in Day One). Then head south on Highway 1 to Monterey.

South of San Francisco, you'll drive on mostly two-lane roads past residential areas of Daly City and Pacifica, by rugged coastal views with substantial drop-offs, by beautiful (and ubiquitous) roadside pampas grass, through laid-back Half Moon Bay, past two nice beaches at San Gregorio and Pescadero, by circa-1871 Pigeon Point Lighthouse, past the cement plant in Davenport, by Northern California's surfing Mecca, and on into Santa Cruz. (See "Alternative Activities" at the end of the prior chapter for things to do in Santa Cruz.)

You'll need to follow the signs carefully in Santa Cruz, especially at Chestnut Street where Highway 1 becomes a divided highway and veers away from the coast. For some distance, you'll see a lot of Brussels sprout, strawberry and artichoke plants, but only a few glimpses of the water. Returning to the oceanfront, you'll continue on Highway 1 through the towns of Moss Landing, Castroville (which produces 95 percent of the nation's artichokes), Marina, and Seaside.

At Moss Landing, look about 100 yards offshore for a dark-blue finger of water. This signals the beginning of the Monterey Canyon, an underwater chasm that's wider and almost three times as deep as Arizona's Grand Canyon—and extends more than twice as far southwest as you can see! We'll talk more about the Monterey Canyon later.

Monterey—California's Capital Before the Gold Rush

When you arrive in Monterey, leave the highway at the Central Monterey/Fisherman's Wharf exit, which empties onto Fremont Street, and after a short distance, turn right onto Camino El Estero. Look for the Monterey Visitor Center on your right—before the road dead-ends at Del Monte Avenue. This is a good place to pick up brochures and ideas if you're going to spend more than a day in the area. When you reach

Del Monte Avenue, turn left and, shortly thereafter, right, into the Fisherman's Wharf/Monterey State Historic Park parking lot. There is a lot to do in this area. You could easily spend the rest of the day here and never get to the primary attractions on our itinerary. So, we've carved out just a portion of Monterey State Historic Park for you to see. Mostly, we suggest that you bypass Fisherman's Wharf, which despite its name, can't hold a candle to its namesake in San Francisco. Unless you plan to go deep-sea fishing or whale watching (December through May), you'll find the wharf to be little more than a collection of shops and restaurants. You'll have access to plenty of those later in Cannery Row.

Instead, we'll take a brief walk-by tour of five historic buildings, and then move directly to Cannery Row for lunch and our visit to the Monterey Bay Aquarium. The five buildings that we'll see here are part of the park's 46 structures along the Path of History, a two-mile self-guided walking tour through Old Monterey; all were built before the California Gold Rush in 1848.

A few facts should help put Monterey into perspective: Spanish explorer Sebastian Viscaino landed here in 1602 and named the area for the count of Monte-Rey. More than a century and a half later, Spain began colonizing California in 1770 after it was learned that the Russians were invading the coast farther north. Father Junipero Serra landed here in that year and built Carmel Mission (which we'll visit this afternoon). Monterey was the capital of California under Spanish rule from 1775 to 1822, when Mexico gained control. On July 7, 1846 Commodore Drake Sloat raised the American flag outside the Custom House during the Mexican-American War. California's constitution was drawn up in Monterey in 1849. (California became a state in 1850). In other words, Monterey was the political, economic and cultural center of California for over 70 years—until the Gold Rush shifted power to the north, and San Francisco became California's number one city.

A Brief Walk-by Tour: Five Historic Buildings

We'll start our walk-by tour at the Pacific House, which faces Custom House Plaza two buildings south of Fisherman's Wharf.

The **Pacific House** is now a visitor center and museum, but beginning in 1847 it was a military supply depot and then a tavern. Of adobe construction (sun-dried bricks made of mud and straw), the first floor of Pacific House contains historic exhibits and the second floor has a collection of Native American artifacts.

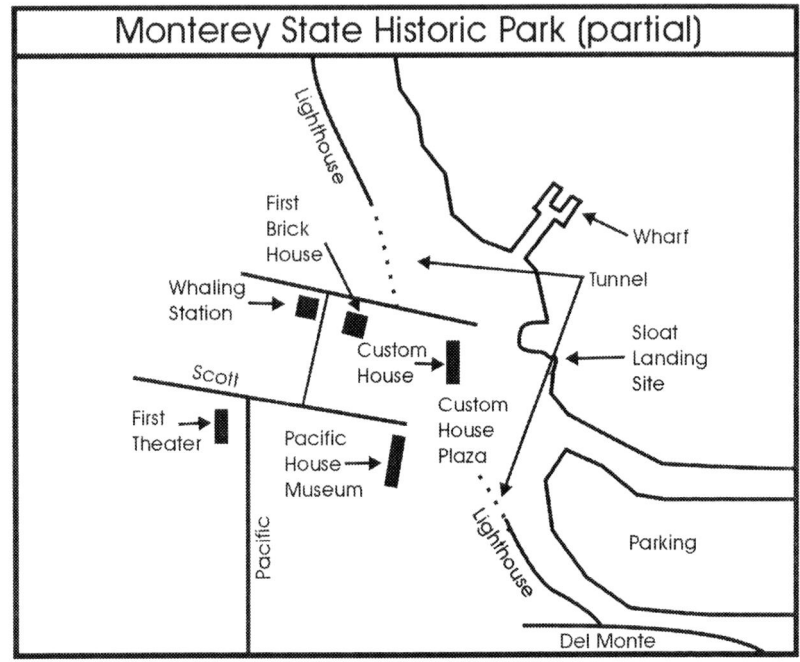

Monterey State Historic Park (partial)

The **Custom House** is one building closer to Fisherman's Wharf. Also adobe, the Custom House was built in 1827 and is the oldest government building on the West Coast. As you've probably assumed from the name, this was the place where all foreign goods shipped into the area were unloaded and duties were collected (until 1867). Inside, you'll see a display of early ship cargo. It was here at the Custom House that Commodore Sloat first raised the American flag in 1846.

From the Custom House, follow the yellow Path of History markers west to the **First Brick House of California**. "Gallant Duncan" Dickenson who had brought a brick-maker with him built it in 1846. Dickenson had been a member of the Donner Party, which suffered grievously after being stranded in the Sierra Nevada Mountains. (More on that during Day Five of our tour.) Dickenson's group split off before the tragedy, so did not suffer with the rest of the Donner group.

The next building west is the **Old Whaling Station**, another adobe, built in 1847 in Scottish architectural style. It was initially a residence, and then housed a whaling business when Gray whales were aggressively fished off Monterey Peninsula between 1855 and 1885. The front sidewalk is unique in that it is made of whale vertebrae pavers.

Now, walk under the archway between the Whaling Station and the First Brick House, through the gardens, and out the back path to the next street. From there, you'll see California's First Theater diagonally to the right.

The **First Theater** was originally a tavern built in 1845 by an English immigrant named Jack Swan. The larger attached structure was built two years later as a boarding house, but was converted to a theater that showed melodramas for $5.00 a person—a hefty entrance fee back then. We suggest that you step inside to see the tavern and theater.

Then, walk two blocks east and you'll be back in Custom House Plaza and on your way to your car.

To get to the Cannery Row parking lot that we recommend, turn right onto Del Monte after exiting the Monterey State Historic Park parking lot, then bear right onto Lighthouse Ave. and drive through the tunnel. About one quarter-mile after exiting the tunnel, you'll come to Foam St., which you'll follow for six blocks to the corner of Foam and Prescott where you'll enter the parking lot. From there, walk downhill two streets to Cannery Row.

Time Check

There are more than 100 businesses in six-block-long Cannery Row. If you love to shop, you could probably spend the rest of the afternoon right here.

We would rather have a quick lunch, visit the Monterey Bay Aquarium, enjoy the 17-Mile Drive, and explore Carmel Mission. The aquarium will take about two hours. The drive from Cannery Row to Carmel Mission (including the 17-Mile Drive) will require an hour and a half. Carmel Mission closes at 5:00 pm.

If you can't make it to Carmel Mission on time, or would prefer to continue your exploration of the coast, you might consider taking in Point Lobos State Reserve, which is described at the end of this chapter under "Alternative Attractions."

It's Lunch Time!

We recommend Louie Linguini's restaurant, which has a beautiful second-floor view of Monterey Bay. This new-ish Italian restaurant has wonderful clam chowder and hearty sandwiches. 660 Cannery Row; 831-648-8500; *www.louielinguinis.com.*

Another fine choice, also with a view of the bay, is The Fishhopper Restaurant. This seafood-and-steak type place serves good sandwiches and salads. 700 Cannery Row; 831-372-8543; www.fishhopper.com.

While you eat, allow us to tell you a little about the Monterey Peninsula, the Monterey Canyon and Cannery Row.

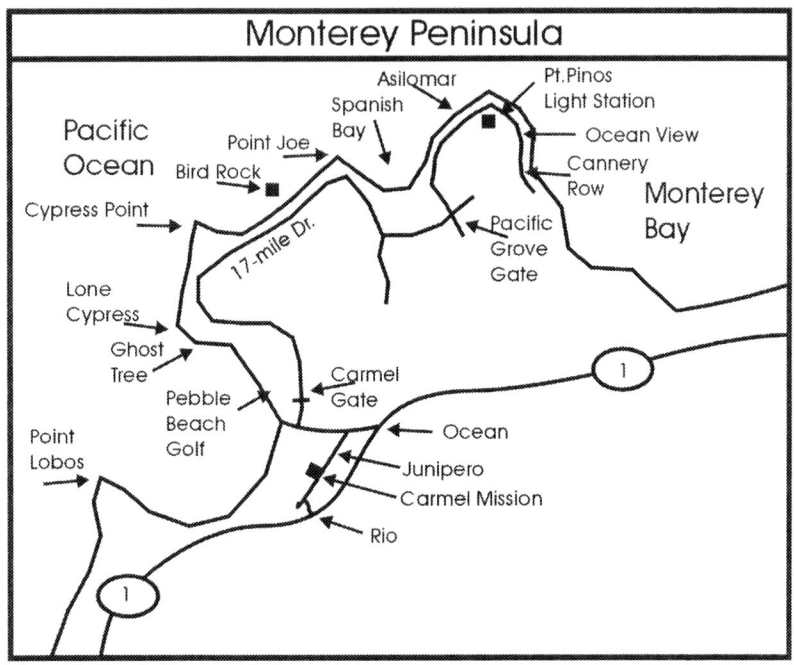

The Peninsula and the Canyon

The 35 square miles of Monterey Peninsula is home to four communities: Pacific Grove in the northwestern tip, best known for its profusion of Monarch butterflies from October to May; Pebble Beach in the west, with its world-famous golf course; Carmel-by-the-Sea in the south; and Monterey in the northeast. Together, they host more than three million visitors a year.

Monterey Bay, extending from Santa Cruz in the north to the western tip of Pacific Grove, is part of the Monterey Bay National Marine Sanctuary. Beginning within the bay at Moss Landing, extending about 65 miles southwest into the Pacific Ocean, and 10,000 feet in depth, is the largest submarine chasm along the western United States and is known as Monterey Canyon. George Davidson discovered it in 1890. This is one of the world's richest marine habitats, caused by upwelling currents from deep within the canyon. The currents bring up an abundance of rich nutrients. This feeds a proliferation of small sea animals and plants that serve as the lowest links in the food chain.

Monterey Bay contains dense kelp beds that are home to sea lions and sea otters; tentacled squid, octopus and jellyfish; bottom-dwelling abalones, crabs, sea urchins, starfish and anemones; and sardines, perch, leopard sharks and all manner of other fish. Gray whales can be seen offshore between December and February during their annual 10,000-mile migration from Alaska to Baja, Mexico, and from March to May during their return trip with newborn calves.

Very shortly, you'll see what this underwater world looks like when you stand in front of the Monterey Bay habitats in the aquarium.

Cannery Row

The rich animal and plant life of Monterey Canyon spawned a major fishing industry here: there was an abundance of sardines in these waters when the first of 18 canneries opened in 1902. However, over-fishing depleted the supply by the late 1940s. (Some 560 million pounds of sardines were processed on Cannery Row in 1945 alone!) During that time, Monterey was known as the "Sardine Capital of the World."

Most sardines were canned, but much of the catch was turned into fishmeal and fertilizer. With all that cooking and processing of fish, you can imagine what the area smelled like back then. In opening his novel, *Cannery Row*, John Steinbeck described the area as "a poem, a stink, a grating noise."

Imagine the fishing boats unloading their catch into floating wooden hoppers and the sardines being sucked ashore into the canneries through large pipes. They were then cleaned, cooked, canned and sent via conveyors to warehouses across 16 bridges that vaulted Ocean View Avenue, now Cannery Row. Two of those original bridges remain.

John Steinbeck lived and wrote in Monterey between 1930 and 1935. If you've read *Cannery Row* and are interested, you'll find Doc Rickett's Western Biological Laboratory at 800 Cannery Row, Lee Chong's market at 835, and the La Ida Cafe at 851.

Monterey Bay Aquarium

You'll find the aquarium, opened in 1984, at the west end of Cannery Row, housed in the old Hovden Cannery. Considered by many to be the finest aquarium in the world, the Monterey Bay Aquarium averages nearly two million visitors a year. Hopefully, you're visiting during a weekday, when the crowds are smaller. On weekends and holidays it's wise to purchase tickets in advance by calling the aquarium at 831-648-4888 inside California, or 800-756-3737 nationwide. Tickets can also be purchased online at the aquarium's Web site (see below).

To us, the forte of this aquarium is that its galleries and exhibits reveal the tremendous variety of sea life that's hidden under water just offshore. The aquarium has 34 major galleries where it displays more than 30,000 creatures in 650 species. About three million gallons of seawater are pumped through the exhibits every day. Do yourself a favor and obtain the visitor map of the aquarium as you enter, and determine where you want to concentrate your energies.

If you enjoy watching animal and fish feedings, consider these: sea otters at 10:30am, 1:30 and 4:00pm; Kelp Forest at 11:30am and 4:00pm; and Outer Bay Exhibit at 11:00am. The sea otters are especially interesting, because they lie on their backs with flat rocks on their stomachs and crack-open shellfish on the rocks.

We particularly enjoyed the two-story-high sea otter tank, the spectacular three-story-high Kelp Forest habitat (visible through a seven inch-thick acrylic window), the Monterey Bay Habitats, the jellyfish gallery, and the million-gallon Outer Bay Exhibit with its sharks, tuna, barracuda, sea turtles, stingrays and other fish swimming behind the largest aquarium window in North America. Also very interesting to us were the shorebirds in the aviary and the touch pools where you can do just that—touch starfish, crabs, bat rays and other underwater creatures.

Open daily, 9:30am-6pm during summer and on major holidays, 10am-6pm the rest of the year; 886 Cannery Row; 831-648-4800; *www.montereybayaquarium.org.*

17-Mile Drive

More than half of the 17-Mile Drive is within the Del Monte Forest. (No, there is no connection with the Del Monte Canning Company.) Since we prefer to show you the coastline up close as much as possible, we'll drive along Pacific Grove's northern and western shores, take in the coastal portion of the 17-Mile Drive and skip the forest.

So, after exiting the parking lot onto Foam St. and heading west two blocks, turn right onto David Ave. and then left onto Ocean View Blvd. Follow Ocean View north until it turns south and becomes Sunset Drive. Along the way, you'll look out onto very picturesque Monterey Bay and the Pacific Ocean.

As you round the northernmost corner of land called Point Piños, you'll see the Point Piños Light Station on your left. Built in 1855, it's the oldest continuously operating lighthouse on the West Coast. It's open Thursday through Sunday, 1-4pm.

Just south of Point Piños is the Asilomar (Spanish for "refuge by the sea") State Beach and Conference Grounds. Begun in 1913 as a YMCA campground and conference site, Asilomar became state property in 1958.

Soon after Sunset Drive turns east, away from the coast, you'll come to the Pacific Grove Gate of the 17-Mile Drive. You'll receive a helpful map as you enter the Drive, but watch your odometer, because signage is not good at the next turn. Nine-tenths (0.9) of a mile after you pass through the gate, turn right onto Spanish Bay Road and return to the coast.

It would be easy to get caught up in the continuing beauty of the 17-Mile Drive's beautiful coastline, seven golf courses and gorgeous homes as you pass by them, but we strongly recommend that you do stop to enjoy and photograph some of the sights. Our favorite points of interest are: Spanish Bay, to enjoy a walk on the beach; Point Joe, where converging currents and submerged rocks cause very turbulent wave action; Bird Rock, to view shore birds and seals; Cypress Point Overlook; The Lone Cypress tree which has withstood Pacific winds and storms for more than 500 years (see the photo at the beginning of this book); and The Ghost Tree, to enjoy the wind- and sea spray-bleached trees and short walking path. If you're a golfer, you'll probably want to see and be photographed at one of the most famous golf clubs in the World, the Pebble Beach Golf Links.

Soon after you pass Pebble Beach, you'll come to the 17-Mile Drive's Carmel Gate. Exit here, drive two blocks ahead, and turn left on Ocean Avenue. At this point, you have two options for getting to Carmel Mission: The first is to drive uphill seven blocks, turn right on Junipero, go eight blocks south to Rio Road, then turn left and follow Rio about a quarter mile until you see the Mission on your right. The second option is to drive all the way to the top of Ocean Ave., and turn right onto Highway 1. After one mile, turn right onto Rio Road and follow that another mile until you find Carmel Mission on your left.

Carmel Mission

The mission was originally begun on the site of the present Presidio Chapel near Monterey Bay and was moved a year later five miles to this location, close to the Carmel River.

By its full name, this is the Mission San Carlos Borromeo del Rio Carmelo, the second of 10 missions founded along the California coast by Franciscan Father Junipero Serra. (The first was founded in San Diego; 11 more were built after Serra's death.) It was also Serra's headquarters and home until he died in August, 1784 at the age of 71. His remains are buried inside the church sanctuary, under the altar.

Although architecturally uninteresting at the front entrance, the mission takes on an aura of 1700s authenticity inside the church and when the mission's carefully restored buildings are viewed from the middle of the plaza. (See the photograph at the front of this book.) The church, with its Moorish-style bell towers, was built of local sandstone and dedicated in 1797; the rest of the mission is adobe. Most of the paintings in the Sanctuary are original to the church. Notice how the walls rise in a steep curve to create a vaulted ceiling.

As you might expect, the purpose of the Mission was to convert the local Ohlone Native Americans to Christianity. About 4,000 were baptized between the mission's founding in 1770 and its conversion (pun intended) to a conventional church in 1834. Between 700 and 1,000 Indians were usually at work in various mission agricultural and construction pursuits; they lived in a nearby village. Some 200 Indians and Spaniards are buried in the mission.

It's our experience that this is a place where you can actually feel your bodily systems slow down and relax. Peace and serenity seem to reign. It begins the moment you enter the grounds from the museum store and continues until you exit. You can feel it as you walk through the gardens, cemetery and plaza; and you can feel it inside the church and museum.

Inside the museum, don't miss: the cenotaph (the large stone coffin-like monument) in honor of Fathers Serra, Lasuen, Crespi and Lopez; Father Serra's library (the first in California) containing the antique books which he brought to the mission; the silver altar pieces (in the vestment room) which he also brought here; his modest living quarters; and the painting depicting the December, 1602 landing at Monterey of Spanish explorer Sebastian Vizcaino.

Open Monday through Saturday 9:30am-5:00pm and Sunday 10:30am-5pm, except Thanksgiving, Christmas and New Year's; 3080 Rio Road; 831-624-3600; *www.carmelmission.org.*

Carmel-by-the-Sea (its official name)

Known far and wide as an "artsy" community (Mary Austin, Upton Sinclair, Sinclair Lewis, Robinson Jeffers and Jack London were prominent here), there are more than 70 art galleries in Carmel. Most have fully-lighted windows that provide enjoyable after-dinner entertainment.

This is a community that welcomes visitors but not urbanization. Local ordinances prohibit house numbers, parking meters, billboards, stoplights, neon signs, franchise restaurants and stores, and postal deliveries (mail must be picked up at the post office). Trees are protected. Home modifications are carefully controlled, and there are no sidewalks or streetlights in residential areas. The result is an aura of quaintness that's rare in California.

By the way, have you noticed all the "firsts" on the Monterey Peninsula: the first government building, the first capitol of California, the first library, the first brick house, and the first theater. Then there's the best aquarium, the largest underwater canyon, and the "sardine capital of the world." All that within 35 square miles!

It's Dinnertime!
- **Casanova** (a favorite of ours), Italian and French cuisine, 5th between San Carlos & Mission, 831-625-0501, *www.casanova restaurant.com*, $$$.
- **EM LE'S** (another favorite), American home-style cuisine, Dolores between 5th and 6th, 831-625-6780, no Web site but do "google" it, $$.
- **The Forge in the Forest Restaurant**, American cuisine, SW Corner of 5th & Junipero, 831-624-2233, *www.forgeinthe forest.com*, $$-$$$.
- **Grill on Ocean Avenue**, California & Asian cuisine, north Ocean between Dolores & Lincoln, 831-624-2569, *www. carmelsbest.com*, $$-$$$.
- **Rocky Point Restaurant**, steaks and fish, on Highway 1, 10 miles south of Carmel (features a stunning view of the Big Sur coastline), 831-624-2933, *www.rocky-point.com*, $$$.
- **Village Corner Restaurant**, Mediterranean and California cuisine, NE Corner of Dolores & 6th, 831-624-3588, *www. carmelsbest.com*, $$-$$$.

Ginnodo-recommended B&Bs/Inns
- **Adobe Inn**, Dolores at 8th, PO Box 4115 Carmel 93921, 800-388-3933, 831-624-3933, fax 831-624-8636, *www.adobeinn. com*, $$-$$$$
- **Carmel Country Inn**, Dolores at 3rd, PO Box 3756, Carmel 93921 800-215-6343. 831-625-3263. fax 831-625-2945. *www. carmelcountryinn.com*, $$-$$$$.

- **Carmel Fireplace Inn**, San Carlos at 4th, PO Box 4082, Carmel 93921, 800-634-1300, 831-624-4862, fax 831-626-1981, *www. carmelfireplaceinn.com*, $$-$$$$.
- **Carriage House Inn**, Junipero between 7th & 8th, PO Box 1900, Carmel 93921, 800-433-4732, 831-625-2585, fax 831-624-0974, *www.innsbythesea.com/carriage-house*, $$-$$$.
- **Coachman's Inn**, San Carlos at 7th, PO Box C-1, Carmel 93921, 800-336-6421, 831-624-6421, fax 831-624-3311, *www. coachmansinn.com*, $$$.
- **Colonial Terrace Inn**, San Antonio & 13th, PO Box 1375, Carmel 93921, 800-345-8220, 831-626-2741, fax 831-626-2715, *www.thecolonialterrace.com*, $$-$$$$.
- **Crystal Terrace Inn**, Carpenter & Valley Way, PO Box 2623, Carmel 93921, 866-466-4980, 831-624-6400, fax 831-624-5111, *www.crystalterrraceinn.com*, $$.
- **Hofsas House**, San Carlos between 3rd & 4th, PO Box 1195, Carmel 93921, 800-221-2548, 831-624-2745, fax 831-624-0159, *www.hofsashouse.com*, $$-$$$.
- **Monte Verde Inn,** Ocean and Monte Verde, PO Box 394, Carmel 93921, 831-624-6046, fax 831-624-6904, no fax, *www.monteverdeinn.com*, $$$-$$$$.
- **Sandpiper Inn By-the-Sea**, 2408 Bay View Ave., Carmel 93923, 800-590-6433, 831-624-6433, fax 831-624-5964, *www. sandpiper-inn.com*, $$-$$$
- **Stonehouse Inn**, 8th between Monte Verde and Casanova, PO Box 2517, Carmel 93921, 877-748-6618, 831-624-4569, no fax, *www. carmelstonehouse.com*, $$-$$$.
- **Vagabond's House Inn**, 4th & Dolores, PO Box 2747, Carmel 93921, 800-262-1262, 831-624-7738, fax 831-626-1243, *www. vagabondshouseinn.com*, $$-$$$.

AAA- or Mobil-recommended Motels/Hotels

- **Best Western Carmel Bay View Inn**, Junipero between 5th & 6th, Carmel 93921, 800-343-1831, 831-624-1831, Fax 831-625-2336, *www.bestwestern.com*, $$-$$$.
- **Best Western Carmel Mission Inn**, 3665 Rio Rd., Carmel 93923, 800-348-9090, 831-624-1841, fax 831-624-8684, *www. carmelmissioninn.com*, $$-$$$$.
- **Horizon Inn & Ocean View Lodge**, Junipero at 3rd, Carmel 93921, 800-350-7723, 831-624-5327, fax 831-626-8253, *www. horizoninncarmel.com*, $$-$$$.

- **Lobos Lodge**, Ocean & Monte Verde, Carmel 93921, 831-624-3874, fax 831-624-0135, *www.loboslodge.com*, $$-$$$.
- **Normandy Inn**, Ocean & Monte Verde, Carmel 93921, 800-343-3825, 831-624-3825, fax 831-624-4614, *www.normandyinn carmel.com*, $$-$$$.
- **Pine Inn**, Ocean between Lincoln & Monte Verde, Carmel 93921, 800-228-3851, 831-624-3851, fax 831-624-3030, *www.pineinn.com*, $$-$$$.
- **Wayside Inn**, Mission & 7th, Carmel 93921, 800-433-4732, 831-624-5336, fax 831-626-6974, *www.innsbythesea.com/way side*, $$$.

Woodall's-recommended Campgrounds
- **Carmel By the River RV Park**, Carmel; from jct. of Hwys 1&68, drive 3 mi. S. on Hwy 1 to Carmel Valley Rd., then 4-1/2 mi. SE to Schulte Rd., then 1 mi. SW on Schulte to entrance on the right; 831-624-9329, *www.carmelrv.com*.
- **Saddle Mountain Recreation Park**, Carmel; same as for Carmel By the River RV Park, except entrance is at the end of Schulte; 831-624-9329.
- **Marina Dunes RV Park**, Marina; from jct. of Hwys 1&156, drive 6 mi. S on Hwy 1 to Reservation Rd., then 1/4 mi. N on Dunes Dr.; 831-384-6914; *www.marinadunesrv.com*.

*****

ALTERNATIVE ATTRACTIONS

During a recent trip to the area, we visited the National Steinbeck Center, Point Lobos and Big Sur (in that order) in a single day of touring. If you can extend your trip to include these worthwhile attractions, we believe you'll enjoy them immensely, as we did. Santa Cruz is also very worthwhile.

The National Steinbeck Center

The Center is located in Salinas, about 22 miles from Monterey, via Highway 68. We came to this birthplace of author John Steinbeck on the strong recommendation of a friend. Between the two of us, we had read only one of Steinbeck's novels, *Cannery Row*. We were so impressed with what we learned about this Pulitzer- and Nobel Prize-winner that we left with an armload of his books, including *The Grapes of Wrath,*

East of Eden, Of Mice and Men, and *Travels with Charley.* The exhibits are engrossing and visually exciting.

The Center also has a wing that tells the story of Salinas Valley agriculture (the Valley calls itself "The Nation's Salad Bowl" because of the wide variety of fruits and vegetables grown there), and a gallery that hosts changing art and cultural exhibits. The 13-minute movie on John Steinbeck is very worthwhile.

Open daily 10am-5pm, except Easter, Thanksgiving, Christmas and New Years Day; One Main Street, Salinas 93901; 831-775-4721 or 831-775-4720 (recording); *www.steinbeck.org.*

Point Lobos State Reserve

Located about three miles south of Carmel on Highway 1, Point Lobos is a 1,250-acre nature reserve with 12 walking trails allowing visitors reasonably close-up observation of coastal plant life, birds and sea animals. Each trail is described on the trail map, which you'll receive at the entrance station. We recommend any of three trails: the Cypress Grove Trail, to see the rare stand of Monterey cypress trees, barking sea lions on the outer rocks, and sea otters in the giant kelp; Sea Lion Point Trail, to see the wonderful view, the turbulent water called Devil's Cauldron, as well as sea lions and sea otters; and Bird Island Trail, to see China Cove Beach, where mother harbor seals nurse their young in April and May, and the large colony of Brandt's cormorants nesting on Bird Island.

All three trails are eight-tenths of a mile or less in length. You might also spot humpback and blue whales offshore, brown pelicans, great blue herons and black-tailed deer. Be careful to avoid the poison ivy bushes which are so prevalent here; its leaves grow in groups of three and have a waxy sheen, and touching anywhere on the plant can cause a blistery red skin rash.

The name Point Lobos, "Point of the Wolves" in Spanish, was named for the resident sea lions.

Open 9am-7pm in summer, 9am-5pm in winter; Route 1, Box 62, Carmel 93923; 831-624-4909; *www.pointlobos.org.*

Big Sur

The 23 miles of coastline between Point Lobos and the village of Big Sur is absolutely gorgeous—and it's part of the California Sea Otter Game Refuge. Unlike Highway 1 from San Francisco to Monterey, most of this drive weaves high above ocean coves and provides many photo opportunities—and sea otter sightings if you have binoculars. (See the photograph at the front of this book.) During the summer months, you may have to take your photographs between breaks in the fog. A natural turnaround point is the small commercial complex on the ocean side of Highway 1 comprising the Nepenthe Restaurant, the Cafe Kevah and the Phoenix shop (the latter is filled with quality one-of-a-kind items). If you want to walk on a Big Sur beach, the place to do it is at Pfeiffer Beach. The road to the beach is 1-1/2 miles north of Nepenthe. Look for the yellow sign, "RVs and Trailers Not Recommended." It's a two-mile drive from Highway 1 down to the beach and there is a parking fee. Is it worth it? Yes, if you like beach walking and watching the ocean crash over rocks and surge through holes in the rocks.

For dinner at a steak-and-fish restaurant with a knock-your-socks-off ocean view (entrees are appropriately priced), try Rocky Point Restaurant (831-624-2933, *www.rocky-point.com*). You'll see it on the west side of the road about 10 miles south of Carmel.

Santa Cruz

The town of Santa Cruz is located on the north end of Monterey Bay, 28 miles from Monterey via Highway 1. Three attractions predominate here: the boardwalk, the Municipal Pier and the Santa Cruz campus of the University of California.

The *piecé de resistance* is the town's old-fashioned boardwalk, with its charming merry-go-round dating from 1911, its Ferris wheel, its many other rides, games, food stands, penny arcades, and the adjoining beach, which is very popular in the summertime. During our early-married years, we traveled to Santa Cruz for only one reason: to ride the Giant Dipper, a circa-1924 wooden roller coaster, over and over again until we'd had enough. We checked it out recently and it's still a great ride!

Across the water from the boardwalk and beach is the Municipal Pier, featuring nice restaurants, fish markets and fishing facilities.

The University of California at Santa Cruz is located on 2,000 acres of redwoods and rolling grasslands high above the city. Take a walk through the woods to see the architecturally innovative campus, and also the view of Monterey Bay from up here.

Just 20 miles north of Santa Cruz, via Highways 9 and 236, is 18,000-acre Big Basin Redwoods State Park, established in 1902. This is the first of the California state parks, and as the name suggests, is a great place to view the giant coast redwood trees while hiking one of its many trails. Hike the half-mile Redwood Trail loop near the park headquarters to see a particularly impressive stand of virgin redwoods.

Day Three - The Valley and Yosemite

If you've already been to Yosemite Valley and want to experience something else, consider our alternative: a tour of Yosemite's Mariposa Grove of Giant Sequoias and a visit to the Pioneer Yosemite History Center.

We strongly recommend that you get underway as early as possible today, in order to maximize your enjoyment of some of the most beautiful mountain scenery in the world: the Yosemite Valley. The drive to Yosemite will take most of the morning.

Here's a quiz question for you. What seven areas of Northern California have made the state famous?

If you answered San Francisco, the Monterey Peninsula, Yosemite, the Gold Country, Lake Tahoe, and the Wine Country, you're correct—but you only got six of the seven answers.

The seventh is the San Joaquin Valley.

A typical reaction of someone who fails this test is, "I've heard of the San Joaquin Valley, but I don't know where it is…And why has it helped make California famous?"

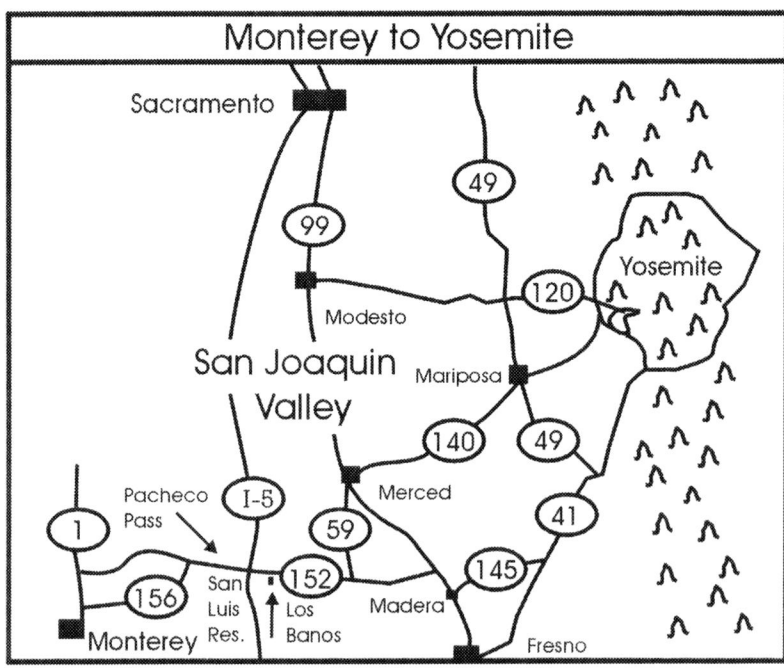

The San Joaquin Valley

After you travel about an hour between the Monterey Peninsula and Pacheco Pass, via Highways 1, 156 and 152, you'll pass the San Luis Reservoir State Recreation Area and then look down into the heart of the San Joaquin Valley. Initially, you may think, "Flat, boring, hot; let's get through this as quickly as possible." But once you learn what we have about the San Joaquin Valley, you may see it differently—and understand why it's famous.

Here it is in a nutshell: It's true that the San Joaquin Valley is flat and hot, especially from May through September. But it produces more than 300 different types of crops each year valued at more than $15 billion—more than 20 percent of America's table food! That's ample justification for its reputation as the most productive agricultural region in the world.   The valley is no longer boring to us, thanks to Dr. James J. Parsons, a professor at our alma mater, the University of California at Berkeley. He was a "cultural geographer," an expert on the geography and human history of the San Joaquin Valley. And he was a man who loved this valley and shared his knowledge both in the classroom and in a lecture titled, "A Geographer Looks at the San Joaquin Valley."

Before we tell you what he said, we'd like to answer the question about where the San Joaquin Valley is situated geographically. It's in the center of the state, in a trough between the Coast Ranges and the Sierra Nevada Mountains. It comprises the southern two-thirds of California's entire Central Valley, which is approximately 50 miles wide and 450 miles long, extending from Redding in the north to the Tehachapi Mountains south of Bakersfield.

The Sacramento Valley, north of the San Joaquin Valley, makes up the rest of the Central Valley.

Here are some pieced-together highlights from Dr. Parsons' lecture. Celia thinks they run on too long; Bill thinks they are all interesting; you can speed-read or skip them if you agree with Celia.

- The southern part of the valley was a barren desert waste with scattered saltbush when first viewed by Don Pedro Fages in 1772, coming from the south over Tejon Pass. Beyond, he could see the tule marshes, fed by streams carrying sierra snowmelt, that for several months each year became the wintering grounds for migrating waterfowl, including Canadian geese, pintails, cinnamon teal and whistling sway. But it was and is dry country. Less than five inches of rain annually falls in southwestern Kern County, maybe ten inches at Fresno.

- The valley's summer heat is intense but dry and so much more tolerable than the stifling humidity of a mid-western July or August. The relatively cool valley nights could scarcely be bought at any price in St. Louis. It is the same heat, of course, that provides such ideal growing conditions for the valley's multitude of crops.
- The first Europeans found a substantial Indian population in the valley. Some have suggested that the density was as great as that of any non-agricultural people in any part of North America. They were village-dwelling Miwok and Yokut who were specialized hunters, fishers and gatherers.
- I happen to like the valley. It's the state's engine-room, where much of the serious work gets done. For me there is a wondrous excitement in the sweeping vistas of fields and orchards. I'm fascinated by the contrast between the endlessly straight roads and the graceful curves of the great federal and state aqueducts, by the vertical silhouettes of the occasional grain elevators, the equipment dealer's yards full of bright-colored John Deere harvesters and J.I. Case tractors, the stately rows of Canary Island palms marking the approaches to some of the older ranch headquarters, the canneries huddled along the tracks in every valley community. Then there are the wineries and their tasting rooms, the farms of meat birds, the Kern County oil fields, and the color, variety and magic of the valley towns themselves (at least some of them), islands of leafy green in the summer, glued to the railroad tracks that were once their lifeblood. Even the Third World barrios of Mexican and Filipino farm workers, a transient population whose economic status is reflected in the untidy but honest and lived-in appearance of houses and yards, help evoke the spirit of place. But most of all the visitor is likely to be caught up with the endless procession of crops, sometimes identified by signs ("apricots," "figs," "wine grapes") erected by a local service club for the benefit of the 'city slickers' who may have their curiosities aroused, by the riot of almond blooms in February, of peaches in March, of orange blossoms redolent with fragrance in April, or the westside's vast ranches of snowy-white cotton bolls in September, the bustle and movement of workers and machines at a harvest time that is different for each crop. One's senses are strained to take it all in.
- Cattle ranching dominated land use at first, later replaced by sheep, trailed each summer to Sierra pastures, and about 1870, by bonanza wheat farming. With the arrival of the San Joaquin Valley Railroad (later the Central Pacific) in the mid-1870's, canal building and

irrigated farming began to take hold. With no woodland to be cleared or heavy sod to be broken it was an 'easy' frontier for settlers.

- Grapes that had been accidentally allowed to dry on the vines in the California Colony near Fresno in 1875 had given rise to an industry [raisins] that soon was to dominate that area.
- The succession of ethnic groups that have supplied the hands to plant, till and harvest the crops of the valley began with the Chinese. When anti-Chinese sentiment intensified, they drifted on toward the cities. The Japanese came next but in the end suffered a similar fate. No ethnic group is more closely tied to one industry than the Portuguese; dairying is largely in the hands of Portuguese from the Azores or their descendants. Other European ethnic groups who are closely identified with particular valley places include the Swedes (Turlock and Kingsburg), the Yugoslavs (Delano), the Dutch (Ripon), Germans (Reedly, Lodi), and the Basques (Bakersfield). Italians and Italian-Swiss are concentrated in the wine industry and in dairying. There are Filipinos in the Delta, Sikhs in Stockton, Russians in Kerman, Assyrians in Modesto and Turlock and Japanese around Livingston.
- The Dust Bowl immigration of the Depression era was of another sort—white Protestant Anglo-Saxons from Texas and Oklahoma, refugees from drought and poverty. The 'Okies' were immortalized by Steinbeck through the image of the Joad family bouncing west in their jalopies along Highway 66 to become migrant pickers at the very bottom of the economic ladder. Today they have 'made it'. First and second generation Okies pretty much run the valley. The black component of the Dust Bowlers is today confined to the larger valley cities.
- It is different with the Mexican-Americans or Chicanos. Since World War II a distinctive Mexican sub-culture has emerged in the valley. The old stock Hispanics, some dating back more than a century, are rarely found in the fields today. It is the newer arrivals from Mexico, whether legal or undocumented, who do the pruning, planting and picking. In each of the valley counties between 20 to 30 percent of the population is Hispanic, with Fresno at the high end.
- To talk of the valley is to talk of agriculture. It could hardly be otherwise when five of the top ten agricultural counties in the US are in the San Joaquin Valley. But this flat, linear world of California's Heartland is somehow outside the American rural farm

tradition. There is no tobacco, no soybeans, no peanuts, and relatively little corn, wheat or even sugar beets. Mixed farming, based on an integration of crops and livestock in which the farmer feeds most of his crops to fattening animals, is unknown. Pigs are a rarity and beef cattle are pretty well confined to the unirrigated higher ground along the valley margins and a few feedlots. The San Joaquin's is a specialty, cash-crop agriculture, in which the product is often perishable and subject to violent and unpredictable market fluctuations. It is dependent on a mobile labor force, adequate irrigation water, a long growing season and relatively rain-free summers.

- Nothing has changed the structure of valley agriculture quite so much as mechanization. Mechanical picking of cotton was in place by 1950. Then came the tomato harvester and the mechanical harvesting of grapes, the vines especially trellised to accommodate the machines.

- Some crops, like almonds and alfalfa, are found almost everywhere. Others are sharply confined to restricted areas such as olives (Lindsay), cherries (Linden), asparagus (the Delta), carrots (Arvin), early potatoes (Shafter), tokay grapes (Lodi), bare-root roses (Wasco) and sweet potatoes (Atwater). Most of the orange growers are in a narrow thermal belt close to the mountains on the east side. Patterson calls itself "the apricot capital of the worked," Mendota "the cantaloupe city." Raisin grapes, chiefly Thompson seedless, are found especially on the sandy soils north and south of Fresno, table grapes around Lodi, Reedley and Delano. Cotton, with more than a million acres, is confined to the southern two-thirds of the Valley.

- Newer crops include safflower, pistachios, persimmons, pome-granates, kiwis, pecans, pineapple, guava, Granny-smith apples, tangerines, corn and avocados.

- The higher sugar content of San Joaquin-grown grapes makes them ideal for sweet wines, raisins and table use and in these markets the valley reigns supreme. Eighty percent of California's grapes and more than half of the total of all grapes grown in the United States are produced in the San Joaquin Valley.

- Fresno is the "agribusiness capital" and the valley's center point. Stockton is the valley's port. Modesto is the food processing capital. Bakersfield is an oil town but also the operational base for some of the state's leading farming corporations.

- So we come back to the humanized landscape, the valley as a dynamic organism, an area to be appreciated for its own sake. The complexity of its patterns and problems, the countless adaptations and human decisions from which it is always evolving, make it a place of excitement and even of subtle beauty and grandeur, one of critical importance for California's present and future society and economy.

Los Banos to Mariposa

So, as you continue on Highway 152 east of Los Banos, you'll see just a very small slice of that greater view of the San Joaquin Valley that Dr. Parsons has shared with us. But we hope you agree with us that seeing the valley through his eyes makes it much more interesting.

Twenty miles east of Los Banos, you have a choice to make: Yosemite Valley or the Mariposa Grove/Pioneer History alternative (see "Alternative Attractions" at the end of this chapter and "Things You Should Know" at the beginning of the book). If you choose Yosemite Valley, turn left on Highway 59, follow it into Merced, then take Highway 140 east toward the park. If you choose the Mariposa Grove of Giant Sequoias and the Pioneer Yosemite History Center, continue on Highway 152 to Highway 99, drive south to Madera, then east on Highway 145 and north on Highway 41 to Yosemite's South Entrance.

Lunch, Gas-Up, and Then Into Yosemite

If you have not yet read the "What You Should Know" section at the front of this book, you should do so before proceeding past Mariposa. Highway 140 may be closed and you may need to select an alternative route.

Since you'll probably be in the vicinity of Mariposa about lunchtime, we have a recommendation for you: the Red Fox Restaurant, at Highway 140 and 12th St. on the north end of town. If you make it all the way to Yosemite Valley by lunchtime, see the restaurant choices below, under "Yosemite Valley Restaurants."

Be sure to check whether your vehicle needs to be refueled in Mariposa. *There are no gas stations in Yosemite Valley.* The last place to gas-up is in El Portal, about 27 miles ahead.

Soon after you leave Mariposa, you'll be driving alongside the Merced River, past the town of El Portal (last chance for gasoline), through Merced Gorge and on into Yosemite National Park at the Arch Rock Entrance.

Here's a tip: if you are a U.S. citizen or permanent resident 62 years of age or older, you're eligible for the Golden Age Pass. It costs only $10.00 and gives you lifetime access to all U.S. National Parks.

About five miles beyond the Arch Rock Entrance, you'll come upon Wawona Road, which is an extension of Highway 41. It's on the west, or near, end of Yosemite Valley. At this junction, we're going to take a short detour that provides a most spectacular introduction to Yosemite Valley.

Turn right on Wawona Road/Hwy 41 and follow it uphill about two miles until just before the Wawona Tunnel, where you'll find a parking lot on the right...and a scene that will take your breath away. (The photograph on the back cover of this book was taken from here.)

Yosemite National Park

As you look at this spectacular scene, we'll give you some sense of the scale, makeup, and geologic history of the Park. It's approximately 37 miles wide by 47 miles long (1,169 square miles) or about the size of Rhode Island. Visitors are primarily attracted to three distinct areas of Yosemite National Park: the Mariposa Grove of Giant Sequoias, the wilderness area, and Yosemite Valley.

The world-famous Mariposa Grove is 36 miles south of Yosemite Valley on Wawona Road/Hwy 41 and features 500 giant sequoia trees within 250 acres of forest. Nearby are the Pioneer Yosemite History Center and the historic Wawona Hotel. All are described under "Alternative Attractions" at the end of this chapter.

Yosemite's wilderness area comprises about 95 percent of the Park, and is accessible primarily via Tioga Road/Hwy 120, which crests the Sierras at Tioga Pass and carries travelers toward Nevada and points east. Open only in the summer, the wilderness area is popular with hikers, backpackers, campers and rock climbers who seek high country environments. Approximately 40 miles north of where you're standing is the Hetch Hetchy Reservoir and O'Shaughnessy Dam (completed in 1923 and a source of San Francisco's drinking water and hydroelectric power).

The Incomparable Yosemite Valley

We think that the Yosemite Valley must be one of the most beautiful places on Earth. Seven miles long and a mile wide, it's rimmed by spectacular granite and waterfall icons that are known throughout the world. From this high vantage point, you can see: El Capitan, the vertical giant on the left; Half Dome, in the middle at the far end of the Valley; triangular-shaped Sentinel Rock; and Cathedral Rocks and Bridalveil Fall on the right. Glacier Point, one of the premier viewing locations in the Park, is barely visible on the ridge behind Sentinel

Rock. We tell you how to get to Glacier Point in "Alternative Attractions," below.

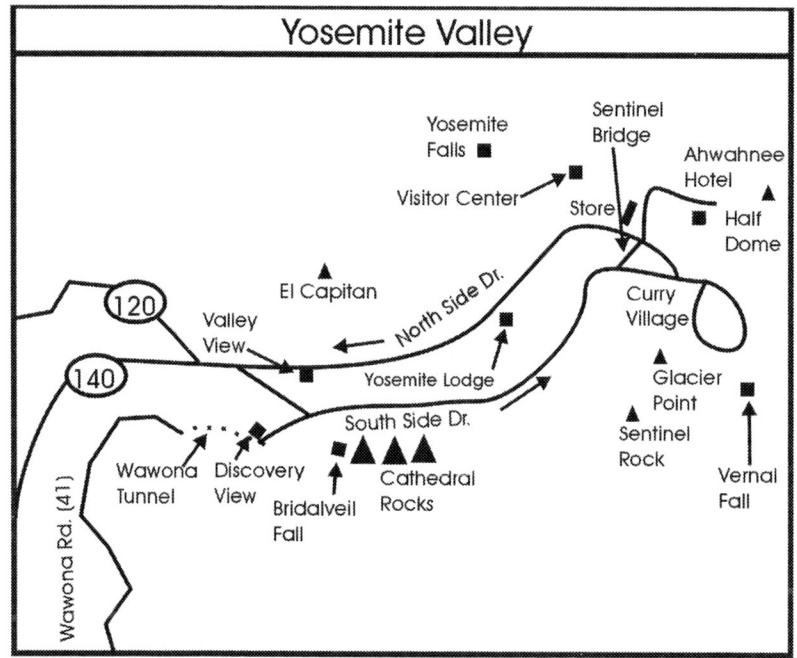

Hidden from view behind El Captain are the famed Yosemite Falls. Hidden by Cathedral Rocks are falls by the names of Sentinel, Illilouette, Vernal and Nevada. We, and numerous other visitors, have enjoyed hiking up Mist Trail to view Vernal Fall from the top.

To give you some sense of scale, the Valley floor sits at 3,960 feet above sea level, the summit of El Capitan is at 7,569 feet, and Half Dome tops out at 8,852 feet. That means El Capitan stretches 3,600 feet above the Valley floor and Half Dome is 4,900 feet high—over three times the tallest building in the world.

Extraordinary scene, isn't it?

Believe it or not, the Valley hasn't always looked like this. All of what you see was once under the ocean. Geologists tell us two collisions of the earth's plates, about 150 and 25 million years ago, forced this part of the continent upward, thereby forming the Sierra Nevada mountain range. That was followed by roughly 22 million years of mountain erosion, as well as canyon carving by rivers and streams. And that was followed by some two to three million years of glaciations.

Yosemite Valley is a classic example of a u-shaped glacial valley. It was originally carved into a v-shape by the Merced River, but was later changed to a u-shape by the downhill movement of a series of glaciers that slowly tore away and ground up the canyon's walls.

Why is the Valley floor flat instead of v-shaped? Because the glaciers deposited a long mound of rock, called a moraine, which blocked this end of the Valley. The last glacier melted about 10,000 years ago and became a lake, which was eventually filled in with 2,000 feet of sediment that washed down from higher regions of the Park.

The glaciers filled most of the Valley, from bedrock 2,000 feet below the current valley floor to the top of Sentinel Rock. That's 6,000 feet, or more than a mile high! And this was just the lead edge of the glaciers; they actually extended about another 30 miles up Tenaya Canyon to the Northeast.

All that tearing away of rocks caused another interesting phenomenon: leaping waterfalls. Streams that had been running down the sloped sides of the canyon, or through small valleys near the tops of rock formations, now drop vertically to the Valley floor. If you look at Bridalveil Fall, you'll see a great example of that. Another dramatic example is Yosemite Falls which, at 2,425 feet, is the fifth highest falls in the world (behind Angel Falls in Venezuela, Tugela Falls in South Africa, and Utigordsfossen and Mongefossen Falls in Norway). Sentinel Fall is the eighth highest of the world's falls.

Yosemite Valley has 13 waterfalls, most of which are best seen in April, May or June, because they're the result of spring snow melt. Unfortunately, the spectacular Yosemite Falls is one that dries up; visitors who come during late summer and fall are often disappointed when they miss seeing this icon of the Valley. Bridalveil Fall, however, is fed by a watershed that holds more water, so it rarely dries up completely.

That, in a nutshell, is the geologic history of Yosemite Valley. What about the human history?

From Miwok Haven to National Park

Anthropologists tell us that Miwok-speaking Native Americans, who called themselves "a-wah-ni-chi," were the primary inhabitants of Yosemite Valley for about 4,000 years before white men arrived. The white men called them "Yosemites," taken from the Miwok word for grizzly bear, "u-zum-a-ti." The Miwok called the Valley "a-wah-ni," which apparently means, "Place like a gaping mouth."

Since you'll soon have the opportunity to learn about the Miwok way of life at the Indian Village and Cultural Exhibit, adjacent to the Visitor Center, we won't comment further on them now, other than to say that Miwok is pronounced "mee-wock."

What we do think you'd like to know now is that a group of white men called the Mariposa Battalion, while on a mission in 1851 to capture and relocate the Miwoks, was the first to enter Yosemite Valley. They entered approximately where you're standing, and were awestruck by the beauty of this place; hence the name Discovery View. This particular vantage point has two other names as well: Tunnel View and Inspiration Point.

After white men occupied the area, preservationists became increasingly upset that the Valley was being developed as farmland with the introduction of livestock, crops and orchards. In 1864, they managed to get the U.S. Congress and President Lincoln to grant the Yosemite Valley and the Mariposa Grove of Giant Sequoias to the State of California, preserving them for public use and recreation. Twenty-six years later, spurred on by naturalist John Muir and magazine editor Robert Underwood Johnson, the U.S. government established Yosemite National Park. Sixteen years after that, in 1906, the Yosemite Valley-Mariposa Grove grant to the State of California was rescinded and those lands became part of the national park.

The U.S. Army managed the park from its establishment in 1890 until the National Park Service was created in 1916. Yosemite was the nation's first national park and has served as a model for all others established since then, and for many around the world.

Facts, Bears, Photos and a Challenge

Just a few more miscellaneous-but-interesting facts and we can move on down to the Valley floor: Yosemite National Park is open year-round, except for Tioga Road and part of Glacier Point Road which are impassable during the winter because of heavy snows. The Park receives approximately four million visitors a year. Elevations in the Park range from 2,000 feet above sea level to more than 13,000 feet.

It's common to see mule deer in Yosemite Valley, but you're cautioned to not feed or touch them. Of particular importance, there are between 300 and 500 black bears in the Park. *Be forewarned: Bears can be very dangerous; keep well away if you see one. Take all food and other scented items to your room at night; do not leave them in your car. If you're staying in tent accommodations, use a coin-operated parking lot storage locker. Dispose of garbage properly.*

Now, take one more look (you did take photographs, didn't you?) and try to imagine the end of a storm over the Valley with sunshine breaking through the clouds. Ansel Adams saw that very thing, right here, when he was photographing Yosemite in the 1920's, '30's and '40's, and captured phenomenal images for all to see. You can enjoy them in the Ansel Adams Gallery near the Visitor Center (and usually find complete calendars of them every autumn).

We think you'll agree that the Discovery View/Tunnel View/Inspiration Point scene is one that will never be forgotten. Yet, the individual icons, such as El Capitan, can be similarly breathtaking when seen from the valley floor.

Here's a challenge for you; we'll call it the "Icon Photo Challenge." During the next few hours, find tree-framed views of Bridalveil Fall, El Capitan, Half Dome, Yosemite Falls and Vernal Fall (if flowing), as well as Valley View (see the preceding map), and take long-to-be-enjoyed pictures...with either your camera or your mind's eye. (In past years, Mirror Lake would have been on this list, but the lake has been silting-in and is mostly a meadow now.)

Your first icon photo opportunity will come at the bottom of the hill.

Bridalveil Fall

So, retrace your drive back on Wawona Road/Highway 41 to the valley floor. Just after you reenter the one-way road leading to the east end of the valley, you'll see a sign on your right pointing to Bridalveil Fall and its parking lot. Follow the short trail to the base of the 620-foot high fall and capture your first Icon Challenge picture.

Bridalveil is especially beautiful in mid-summer when the water volume is somewhat less and the breeze causes it to fan out and fall softly to the small pool and boulders below.

Seeing the Valley Floor

Next, take Southside Drive, the one-way road heading east, to find your second icon to photograph. You can't miss it.

Wow!! Isn't that view of El Capitan spectacular?

You'll remember that we said El Capitan stretches 3,600 feet above the valley floor. That's the equivalent of a 360-story building—if there were such a thing. This is the largest single block of exposed granite in the world.

Yet, as hard as it is to imagine, experienced rock climbers actually scale that sheer face and live to tell the story! They do it in about three to seven days, depending upon the route taken. Often, climbers can be seen on the mountain face.

To view and photograph the remainder of these famous icons/sights, you have four choices of approach, and we recommend them in this order:

1) Take an open-air tram on Yosemite Valley Tours. The tour is two hours long, stops for gawking and picture taking, and is Park Ranger-narrated (except in inclement weather when buses are used and the drivers narrate). There is no fixed schedule, but there are numerous departure times each day, from Yosemite Lodge year-round and also from Curry Village during the summer. It's definitely worth the $22 fare.   While it is sometimes possible to purchase tickets on the same day, advance reservations are recommended. To reserve, call 209-372-1240 if within seven days of your visit, or 559-252-4848 if reserving more than seven days in advance.

2) Take the free shuttle bus (approximately one hour to make the circuit if you don't get off, but you will want to). Advantages: it's free; you don't need a reservation; it stops so you can get off, and then back on a following bus about ten minutes later; and it has access to roads (for example, to Mirror Lake) where automobiles are not allowed. Disadvantages: you don't get narration by a knowledgeable person, nor up-close views of sites in the western end of the Valley, because Yosemite Falls is the farthest west the shuttle travels. Pick up a copy of *Yosemite Today* newspaper at the Valley Visitor Center for a map of the shuttle service.

3) Rent bicycles at either Yosemite Lodge (209-372-1208) or Curry Village (209-372-8319). They're the old single-speed type, but helmets and a map of the 8.7-mile Yosemite Valley bike loop path are included.

4) Use the preceding map as your guide to drive to the sites that interest you. We place this option fourth, because you've just spent half a day in the car, and we believe you'll enjoy one of the other options more.

So, we're going to make the assumption that you'll take either a Yosemite Valley Tour or the free shuttle. If you've made a reservation for the tour, you already have a departure time and location. If not, you can either try to purchase a ticket at the booth outside the Village Store, or board the free shuttle. Either way, we recommend that you head for Yosemite Village, which you can reach by continuing east on Southside Drive, to the stop sign (just past the circa-1879 Chapel), crossing

Sentinel Bridge, turning right at the next stop sign, entering the day-use parking lot and walking north. The Village and Village Store will be on your left. Or, if this day-use parking lot is filled, recross Sentinel Bridge and drive to the day-use parking lot at Curry Village, where you can catch the shuttle bus back to Yosemite Village.

By the way, if you drive slowly across Sentinel Bridge, you'll see one of the classic photo opportunities of Half Dome. (The photograph of Half Dome at the front of this book was taken from this bridge.)

The Valley Visitor Center and Environs

The Valley Visitor Center is hidden at the back of Yosemite Village, and you have to search for it, but you'll be amply rewarded when you do find it.

To get there, from the short-term parking lot, walk around the Village Store—or through the store and out the rear door. Then, turn right, walk about the length of a football field, pass the Main Post Office (there are others at Yosemite Lodge and Curry Village), pass the Wilderness Store and Ansel Adams Gallery, and you'll see the Valley Visitor Center on your right.

We have five recommendations for you here: First, see the 20-minute film, *Spirit of Yosemite*, in the theater. Second, look at the displays in the interpretive center and learn more about the geology of Yosemite Valley. Third, visit the Indian Village behind the Yosemite Museum and the Visitor Center to learn about the Miwok and their culture. Fourth, browse around the bookstore where you'll find the best collection anywhere of Yosemite-related literature. (We strongly recommend *The Complete Guidebook to Yosemite National Park*, by Steven P. Medley, if you want additional helpful information during your visit.) And fifth, especially if you plan to use the shuttle, ask a park ranger at the information desk for copies of *Yosemite Today* and the *Yosemite Guide*.

The Valley Visitor Center is open daily 9am-7pm; 209-372-0298; *www.nps.gov/yose* or *www.yosemite.org*.

Other interesting attractions in the immediate area include: the Yosemite Museum, with it's gallery of landscape paintings; the Indian cultural exhibit and store; and the Ansel Adams Gallery, featuring the famous photographer's works and offering photography supplies and gift items.

A short walk to the east, past the Village Store and the Medical Clinic, would bring you to the Ahwahnee Hotel, which was built in 1927 and is a now a National Historic Landmark. To get on with the

Icon Photo Challenge, we suggest that you bypass this for now, and if your budget and wardrobe permit, consider the Ahwahnee for dinner this evening. The dining room's wonderful ambiance and excellent food are bound to please you (see below).

Yosemite Valley Restaurants

After you've seen the highlights of Yosemite Valley, and checked into your accommodations, you'll be ready for some sustenance. All of the valley's food establishments are listed below. If you're dining and sleeping outside the valley, your desk clerk, concierge, or innkeeper should have recommendations.

The Ahwahnee

* **Ahwahnee Dining Room**; traditional, five-star fine dining in a grand old-world ambiance; coats and ties are preferred and advance reservations are suggested; open year-round; breakfast 7-10:30 am, Lunch 11:30am-3pm; Sunday brunch 7am-3pm, Dinner 5:30pm-9pm; $$$-$$$$; 209-372-1489.
* **The Ahwahnee Bar**; cozy, with appetizers and light bar fare; open year-round, 11am-11pm; $$.

Yosemite Village

* **Degnan's Delicatessen**; next to the Main Post Office; sandwiches, salads and snacks; open year-round, 7am-6pm; $-$$.
* **Degnan's Cafe**; hamburgers, chicken, ice cream; open spring through fall, 7am-5pm; $.
* **The Loft at Degnan's**; pizza, salads and appetizers; open spring through fall, Monday-Thursday, 5-9pm and Friday-Sunday, 12 noon to 9pm; $$.
* **Village Grill**; hamburgers, sandwiches, chicken strips, fries, milkshakes; open spring through fall, 11am-5pm, $.

Yosemite Lodge

* **Food Court**; many food choices; open year round; breakfast 6:30-11am, lunch 11:30am-2pm, dinner 5-9pm, light fare served all day; $.
* **Mountain Room Lounge**; sandwiches, salads, appetizer plates; open year-round, Monday-Friday 4:30-10:30pm; $-$$.
* **Mountain Room Restaurant**; fine dining, advance reservations recommended; steak, fish and pasta dishes with views of

Yosemite Falls; outside seating available; open year-round for dinner only, 5:30-10pm; $$-$$$.

Curry Village
- **Coffee Corner**; boxed lunches and baked goods; open year-round, 6am-10pm; $.
- **Pavilion Buffet**; hot entrees, taco bar, stir fry, pasta, salads, soups; open March through October; breakfast buffet 7-10am, dinner buffet 5:30-8pm; $-$$.
- **Pizza Patio;** pizza and salads; open spring through fall, noon to 10pm; $-$$.
- **Taqueria**; Mexican food; open spring through early fall, 11am-5pm; $-$$.

Groceries can be purchased at: the Village Store (8am-9pm); Degnan's Delicatessen (8am-6pm) in Yosemite Village; the Yosemite Lodge Gift/Grocery (8am-9pm); and, in Curry Village, the Gift/Grocery (8am-9pm) and Housekeeping Camp (8am-8pm).

Accommodations in Yosemite Valley
We can't overemphasize the need to make reservations well in advance of your arrival if you want to stay overnight in Yosemite Valley. (See "What You Should Know About Costs, Reservations and Yosemite" at the front of this book.)

There is a single reservation system for all in-park lodging. Contact Delaware North Company Parks and Resorts, 5410 East Home, Fresno, CA 93727; 559-252-4848, or TDD 559-255-8345, *www.yosemite park.com.*
- **The Ahwahnee Hotel** - Luxury in the grand style, also offers several cottages; near Yosemite Village; open year-round; $$$.
- **Yosemite Lodge** - Moderately priced lodge and standard rooms; near Yosemite Falls; open year-round; $$.
- **Curry Village** - This is the least-expensive option in Yosemite Valley; motel rooms with bath, cabins with bath, cabins without bath, and canvas tent cabins without bath; open from spring to fall and on holidays and weekends in winter; $$.

When Yosemite Valley Accommodations are Unavailable
As we said in the "What You Should Know" section at the front of this book, overnight accommodations in Yosemite Valley are very difficult to obtain during tourist season and on many weekends

throughout the year. *It's best to make your reservation well in advance and cancel it (for a full refund, at least seven days before your arrival) if you can't make it on that date.*

The following lists of bed & breakfasts, hotels, and motels on Highways 120, 140 and 41 may be of help if you need to make outside-the-park reservations. As with all other establishments listed in this book, we provide Web site addresses for your convenience. Some Web sites provide availability information by date, and will accept reservations online. Don't forget to ask about AAA, AARP or other discounts you may qualify for!

Here are some considerations if you need to find accommodations outside Yosemite Valley:

Very Important: If you want to have dinner and spend your evening hours in Yosemite Valley, you should arrange for late arrival where you'll be staying overnight. Many establishments will release rooms to others if guests do not arrive by 6:00 p.m.

Accommodations on Highway 120, northwest of Yosemite Valley, would be the most convenient, because that's the direction you'll take tomorrow morning on the way to the Gold Country. Groveland, where most of the lodgings on Highway 120 are located, is 45 miles from Yosemite Valley; Evergreen Lodge is much closer to the Park.

The "Close-by Accommodations on Highway 140" would be the most convenient if you were staying more than one night in the area.

Accommodations on Highway 41, some 40 miles south of Yosemite Valley, may be the most convenient if you'll be visiting the Mariposa Grove and Pioneer Yosemite History Center instead of Yosemite Valley.

The most inconvenient lodgings, but sometimes the only ones available (assuming the road is open), are located in Mariposa, 36 miles from the west entrance of Yosemite National Park.

Groveland Area Accommodations on Highway 120

- **All Seasons Groveland Inn**, 18656 Main St., Groveland 95321, 800-595-9993, 209-962-0232, fax 209-962-0250, *www.all seasonsgrovelandinn.com*, $$.
- **Alpenglow Bed & Breakfast at Manzanita Hill**; 19210 Highway 120, PO Box 409, Groveland 95321, 209-962-4541, fax 209-962-6968, *www.manzanitahill.com*, $$-$$$.
- **Blackberry Inn**, 7567 Hamilton Station Loop at Buck Meadows, PO Box 1064, Groveland 95321, 888-867-5001, 209-962-4663, *www.blackberry-inn.com*, $$.

- **The Berkshire Inn**, 19950 Highway 120, PO Box 207, Groveland 95321, 888-225-2064, 209-962-6744, *www.berk shireinn.net,* $$.
- **Evergreen Lodge at Yosemite**, 33160 Evergreen Rd., Groveland 95321, 800-93-LODGE, 209-379-2606, fax 209-391-2390, *www.evergreenlodge.com,* $$-$$$.
- **Groveland Hotel**, 18767 Main St. (Highway 120), PO Box 289, Groveland 95321, 209-962-4000, fax 209-962-6674, *www.groveland.com,* $$-$$$.
- **Hotel Charlotte**, 18736 Main St. (Highway 120), PO Box 787, Groveland 95321, 209-962-6455, fax 209-962-6254, *www. hotelcharlotte.com,* $$.

Close-by Accommodations on Highway 140
- **Cedar Lodge**; 8 miles west of Yosemite entrance; 9966 Highway 140, PO Box C, El Portal 95318; 210 rooms, 2 restaurants, pools; 888-742-4371, 209-379-2612, fax 209-379-2712; *www.yosemitemotels.com/cedarlodge;* $$.
- **Yosemite View Lodge**; just outside the park boundary; 11136 Highway 140, PO Box D, El Portal 95318; 278 rooms, 2 restaurants, pools; 888-742-4371, 209-379-2681, fax 209-379-2704; *www.yosemitemotels. com/yosemiteviewlodge;* $$-$$$.

Mariposa-Area Accommodations on Highway 140
- **Best Western Mariposa**, 4999 Highway 140, PO Box 1989, Mariposa 95338, 888-742-4371, 209-966-7545, fax 209-966-6353, *www.bestwestern.com,* $.
- **Boulder Creek Bed & Breakfast, Mariposa**, 4572 Ben Hur Rd., Mariposa 95338, 209-742-7729, no Web site but check Google, $$.
- **Highland House Bed & Breakfast Inn**, 3125 Wild Dove Lane, Mariposa 95338, 209-966-3737, *www.highlandhousebandb. com,* $$.
- **Little Valley Inn,** 3483 Brooks Rd., Mariposa 95338, 800-889-5444, 209-742-6204, fax 209-742-6227, *www.littlevalley.com,* $$.
- **Poppy Hill Bed and Breakfast**, 5218 Crystal Aire Dr., Mariposa 95338, 800-587-6779, 209-742-6273, *www.poppyhill. com,* $$.

- **Restful Nest Bed & Breakfast**, 4274 Buckeye Creek Rd., Mariposa 95338, 800-664-7127, phone & fax 209-742-7127, *www.restfulnest.com*, $$.
- **EC Lodge Yosemite**, 5180 Jones St., Mariposa 95338, 866-325-6343, 209-742-6800, fax 209-742-6719, *www.eclodge yosemite.com*, $.

Accommodations on Highway 41

- **Apple Blossom Inn Bed & Breakfast**, 44606 Silver Spur Trail, Ahwahnee 93601, 888-687-4281, 559-642-2001, *www. appleblossominn.com*, $$-$$$.
- **Big Creek Inn Bed & Breakfast**, 1221 Highway 41, PO Box 39, Fish Camp 93623, 559-641-2828, fax 559-641-2727, *www. bigcreekinn.com*, $$-$$$.
- **Comfort Inn Oakhurst**, 40489 Highway 41, Oakhurst 93644, 800-424-6423, 559-683-8282, fax 559-658-7030, *www.choice hotels.com*, $-$$.
- **The Homestead Cottages**, 41110 Road 600, Ahwahnee 93601, 800-483-0495, 559-683-0495, fax 559-683-8165, *www.home steadcottages.com*, $$-$$$.
- **Hound's Tooth Inn**, 42071 Highway 41, Oakhurst 93644, 559-642-6600, fax 559-658-2946, *www.houndstoothinn.com*, $$.
- **Sierra Woods Bed & Breakfast**, 49522 Road 426, Oakhurst 93644, 888-246-0720, 559-642-6248, *www.sierrawoodsbandb. com*, $-$$.
- **Tenaya Lodge at Yosemite**, 1122 Highway 41, Fish Camp 93623, 888-514-2167, 559-253-2005, *www.tenayalodge.com*, $$$-$$$$.
- **Yosemite's Sierra Mountain Lodge** (B&B), 45046 Fort Nip Trail, Ahwahnee 93601, 559-683-7673, *www.sierramountain lodge.com*, $$.

Campgrounds

There are three drive-in and one walk-in campgrounds in Yosemite Valley, and nine other campgrounds elsewhere within the park (including Wawona, if you're headed there). Reservations are required year-round and are made on a first-come first-served basis. Contact the National Park Reservation Service, as early as possible, at 800-436-7245, or online at *www.reservations.nps.gov,* or at P.O. Box 1600, Cumberland, MD 21502. International callers use 301-722-1257. For more information call the park campgrounds office at 209-372-8502 or access *www.nps.gov/yose/trip/camping.htm.* The U.S. Forest Service Operates nearby campgrounds on a seasonal basis. Contact district offices: for the Highway140 area, 209-966-3638; for the Highway 41 area, 559-683-4636; for the Highway 120 area, 209-962-7825.

Woodall's-recommended campgrounds

- **Moccasin Point**, Groveland; drive 2 mi. N on Hwy 49 from jct with Hwy 120 to Jacksonville Rd.; 209-852-2396; *www.donpedrolake.com.*
- **Mariposa Fair Grounds**, Mariposa; from jct Hwys 49&40, drive 2 mi. S on Hwy 49; 209-966-2432; *www.mariposa fair.com.*
- **High Sierra RV Resort**, Oakhurst; drive 1/2-mi. NE on Hwy 41 from jct. with Hwy 49; 877-314-7662, *www.highsierrarv. com.*

*****

ALTERNATIVE ATTRACTIONS

Glacier Point

Here's the informative but understated National Park Service description of this attraction:

"Glacier Point, an overlook with a commanding view of Yosemite Valley, Half Dome, and the Sierra Nevada, is located 30 miles (a 1-hour drive) from Yosemite Valley. The view from Glacier point provides an opportunity to see the Valley from its rim.

"From Yosemite Valley, take the Wawona Road (Highway 41) 14 miles to the Chinquapin junction, then turn left onto Glacier Point Road. The road ends at Glacier Point. Glacier Point Road is generally open from late spring through late fall. In winter the road is plowed only as far as the Badger Pass Ski Area, and then Glacier Point can be reached via skis or snowshoes only."

Is it worth the 60-mile round trip drive? Definitely, yes; especially at sunrise and during the late afternoon-evening hours. "Magnificent," "spectacular," "dramatic," "not to be missed" are often used to describe this view 3,214 feet above Yosemite Valley and its broader context, the Sierra Nevada mountains, stretching nearly as far as the eye can see.

Wawona Area

We love the Wawona area of Yosemite National Park. We believe that you, too, will find the Sequoias in the Mariposa Grove to be stunning, and the Pioneer History Center to be very interesting.

To get there, you have two choices: drive to Yosemite National Park via Merced and Mariposa on Highway 140, enter at the Arch Rock Entrance, then drive 36 miles (1-1/4 hours) south on Wawona Road/ Highway 41 (with this first choice, you may want to stop and admire the splendor of Discovery View); or drive through Madera and Oakhurst via Highways 145 or 41, enter the Park at the South Entrance, and continue two miles to the Mariposa Grove. The Pioneer Yosemite History Center is two miles farther north.

Mariposa Grove of Giant Sequoias

What's a Sequoia? It's just the largest living thing on earth. (Its sister tree, the Redwood, is taller but slimmer and less bulky.) So, here's your opportunity to take a one-hour guided open-air tram tour of a 250-acre forest of 500 giant evergreens and be awed by the immensity and beauty of these trees. Or, if you'd rather walk, there are free trail brochures available in the tram boarding area printed in English, French, Japanese and Spanish.

Trams depart, except during winter, approximately every 20 minutes from 9am to 4pm and cover a five-mile loop in about an hour. There are several stops along the way: Grizzly Giant, which is 96 feet around at the base, 209 feet tall and about 2,700 years old; Tunnel Tree, through which tourists used to drive during the Grove's early days; and the Mariposa Grove Museum.

Pioneer Yosemite History Center

You can see a collection of historic buildings brought together from elsewhere in the park, each of which is described by markers, but you can also take a stagecoach ride, see a collection of old horse-drawn vehicles, cross the North Fork of the Merced River on a circa-1870 covered bridge, and observe a blacksmith at work. Pick up a copy of the self-guided tour brochure at the north end of the covered bridge.

Wawona Hotel

The Victorian 104-room Wawona Hotel, built in 1879 and located adjacent to the Pioneer Yosemite History Center, is a National Historic Landmark. So, it's a logical place for you to eat and sleep; but before you make reservations, we suggest that you view recent traveler comments on *www.tripadvisor.com.* The hotel was undergoing renovations when we last checked the comments and they were not very complimentary. Reservations for accommodations can be made via 866-875-8456 or *www.nationalparkreservations.com.* Dinner reservations can be made at 209-375-1425.

See "Accommodations on Highway 41," above, for places to spend the night outside the south gate of Yosemite. There is a campground in Wawona. See "Campgrounds," above, for reservation information.

Day Four – The Gold Country

If you've previously been to the Gold Country, you may want to see instead: Railtown 1897 State Historic Park, the quaint town of Murphys, the Ironstone Vineyards, Calaveras Big Trees State Park and Indian Grinding Rock State Historic Park, or, spend the day exploring the fine museums in Sonora, Angels Camp, San Andreas, Placerville, and Coloma. These alternative attractions are briefly described within the following text, when they are geographically close to our tour route.

Today, we're going to take a trip back in time...to the mid-1800's, when this small slice of earth was the center of worldwide attention: The Gold Rush! The Mother Lode! California or Bust!

But we know how you must feel now, bedazzled by the magic of Yosemite Valley...and gold mining just doesn't seem to compare. You're going to have difficulty extricating yourself from this very special place. It isn't every day that you can wake up in the midst of such stunning scenery! Fortunately, the 50-mile drive out Highway 120 to Highway 49 is just short of spectacular itself, and the Gold Country will be as fascinating as Yosemite was arresting. So, let's peel ourselves away from Yosemite Valley as early as we can (this is quite a full day), and turn our attention to the interesting experiences that lie ahead.

By the way, the large red-barked bush with gray-green leaves that you'll see in such abundance along Highway 120 is called Manzanita.

This morning and early afternoon, we'll visit three historic towns, concentrating on the centerpiece of our day: Columbia, "The Gem of the Southern Mines." Then, we'll take a two-hour drive up Highway 49 to Placerville, through lovely foothills, learning about other Gold Country towns and happenings along the way.

We'll learn about the Mother Lode and various mining techniques. We'll see Gold Rush architecture, mining equipment and artifacts. And we'll meet some very interesting historical characters.

We probably will not have time to reach Coloma where the Gold Rush started on January 24, 1848, when James W. Marshall discovered the precious metal at Sutter's Mill (see "Alternative Attraction #11," below). But if it's important that you visit this historic place, you can either skip an attraction or two that we suggest, or spend additional time in the Gold Country.

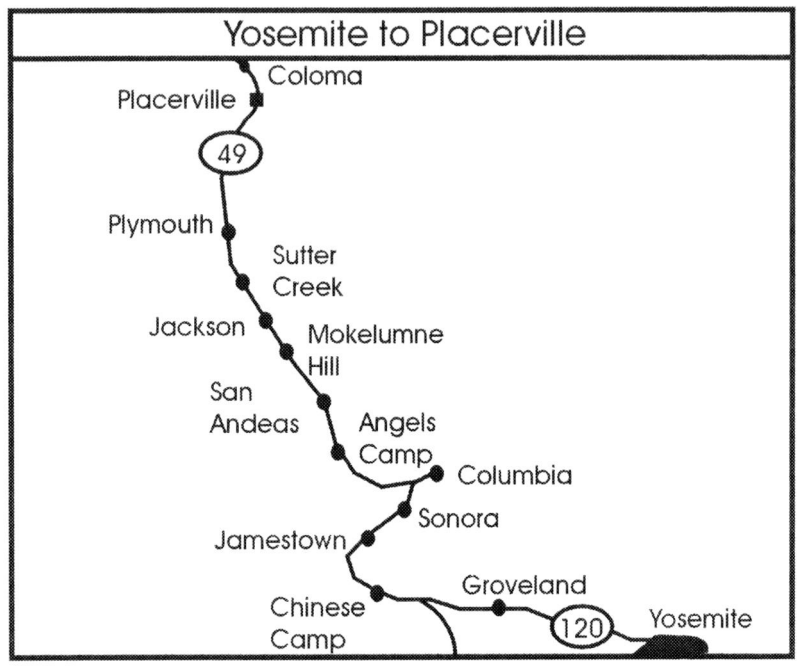

Yosemite to Placerville

Coloma
Placerville
49
Plymouth
Sutter
Creek
Jackson
Mokelumne
Hill
San
Andeas
Angels
Camp
Columbia
Sonora
Jamestown
Groveland
Chinese
Camp
120
Yosemite

Here's a caution based upon our personal experience: in the Gold Country, we're like cats on a beach, wanting to stop and explore every road, every town, every structure...every thing. We've found that it takes a lot of discipline to pass by many things so appealing. Of course you may have interests that differ from ours and you should feel free to deviate from our suggestions. Exploring is great fun.

We've selected three towns for you to visit that should give you a well-rounded experience of the Gold Country...and get you into our evening's destination, Placerville, at a reasonable time. The towns we plan to visit are: Jamestown, Sonora, and Columbia. We'll tell you about others as we drive through or past them.

Historians tell us that there were once 536 mining towns in the Gold Country. They ranged in elevations from roughly 700 feet to 2,500 feet. Remnants of more than 200 gold towns remain, and we'll see some of the prominent ones today.

The term "Mother Lode" refers to the series of gold-bearing "source veins" that were deposited along this stretch 65 million years ago when the Sierras were thrust upward and molten gold was forced through fissures to the surface of the earth. Technically, the Mother Lode, also known as the Southern Mines District, stretches 135 miles south from Auburn to Coarsegold, while the area north of Auburn is known as the Northern Mines district.

Over time, erosion carried flecks of the surface gold from the "source veins" into the streams where it lay awaiting discovery in 1848 by James Marshall, and by thousands of prospectors who would descend upon the area soon after. Some of the flecks, usually called "gold dust," gathered at bends in the streams and downstream from rapids, to form gold nuggets.

At first, gold was so plentiful that the miners merely "panned for gold" (they scooped gravel and sand from the streams into a tin pan and swirled-out everything until only the heavier gold flecks and nuggets remained). However, with more than 300,000 men working the goldfields, it didn't take long for the streams to be panned-out, and new methods were needed in order to get to the deeper gold.

Next came rockers, sluices and long toms, wooden contraptions into which the miners shoveled stream gravels. Essentially the same technique as panning but on a larger scale, water was forced through these devices to wash away the gravel and dirt, again leaving gold behind. On a still larger scale were the barge dredges that floated on dammed-up sections of stream and scooped up everything down to bedrock.

When the easily reached gold was gone, the miners went after it with a vengeance by channeling water from higher elevations through ditches and wooden flumes (troughs) to a hose and nozzle, called a "monitor." This way they could wash whole hillsides into sluices where the gold could be gathered.

After individuals and teams of miners had uncovered most of the surface gold, mining companies were formed to drill shafts deep underground to find and follow the veins. But the high cost of extraction from underground mines ended most gold mining in California by the early 1940's.

The last great hardrock mine to close in California, in the year 1956, was Grass Valley's Empire Mine. It reached a depth of 11,000 feet (over two miles deep) and had 360 miles of tunnels! In 107 years of operation, the Empire Mine produced $70 million in gold.

Lumping it all together, at $16 an ounce, the Gold Rush resulted in the extraction of approximately $2 billion in gold from Coarsegold to Vinton. At today's valuation, that's more than $50 billion!

By the way, we assume that you've made the connection by now: prospectors of the Gold Rush of 1849 were dubbed "49ers," and most of today we'll be driving on...Highway 49.

Chinese Camp

Just a few miles after leaving Highway 120 and entering Highway 49, the first gold town we'll come to is Chinese Camp. There's not much to see here, even though some 5,000 gold-seekers from China lived and worked in these diggings. So we suggest that you drive on by.

Founded in 1849, Chinese Camp became the largest Chinese settlement outside of Asia. Most Chinese gravitated here after being expelled from other diggings by Caucasians, but they worked hard and discovered several major veins in the area. In September 1856 a disagreement between two rival tongs resulted in a 2,100-person rumble; four deaths and a few dozen wounded resulted. The reason there were so few casualties is that few guns were used and the law broke it up.

Jamestown

Six miles beyond Chinese Camp, you'll come to Jamestown. We suggest that you turn right onto Main Street, find a parking place, and take a walk up and down the short street. Feast your eyes on these wonderful false-front stores, overhanging balconies and boardwalks.

Referred to locally as "Jimtown," this is one of the first camps founded in the Gold Country and is best known for its Old West ambiance and the discovery of a 75-pound gold nugget in August of 1848. The Jamestown area really boomed with underground hardrock mining in the late 1890's. In 1984, after a construction crew repaired a damaged sewer pipe on Main Street and dug up several small nuggets, the town was inundated with gold seekers for several days.

High Noon, The Virginian, and *Dodge City* are among the films for which Jamestown has been used as a movie set.

*****

ALTERNATIVE ATTRACTION #1

Railtown 1897 State Historic Park

If you have a serious interest in trains, you may want to visit **Railtown 1897 State Historic Park**. The Park is immediately to the right as you leave Jamestown's Main Street and head north on Highway 49. (We'll be visiting Railtown's parent, the California State Railroad Museum in Old Sacramento on Day Six.) Railtown features lots of steam engines and displays the original roundhouse and workshops of the Sierra Railway, which began shuttling supplies between the San

Joaquin Valley and the foothills in 1897. It also offers a train ride through the foothills, which we found to be great fun. Railtown's locomotives and railcars were used in more than 200 films, TV shows and commercials between 1917 and 2003.

Open daily from 9:30am-4:30pm, April through October, and 10am-3pm, November through March; corner Fifth Ave. & Reservoir Road, PO Box 1250, Jamestown 95327; 209-984-3953; *www.csrmf. org/railtown.*

*****

Sonora

Follow the Columbia State Park and Angels Camp signs to our second stop, Sonora, just three miles north of Jamestown.

Sonora has a much different "feel" than Jamestown. This is a bustling place of 5,000 residents that offers a full range of facilities, including hospitals and shopping centers (in the newer, East Sonora). It was once an important provisioning center for the Gold Country and is today both a commercial center for the area and the seat of government for Tuolumne County. (Pronounced "twallomee.")

After entering Old Sonora on Hwy 49/Stockton St., turn left onto Washington St. and find a place to park (on Washington or one of the side streets). Similar to Jamestown, we suggest that you walk six blocks north on Washington from Stockton to Elkin St. Here, you'll see a mix of old and newer architectural styles, but the general ambiance is decidedly Gold Country. You may even find a boutique, gallery or specialty shop that catches your eye.

Along the way, you'll notice that Old Sonora is positioned in a pretty, narrow valley, which has as its centerpiece the striking red **St. James Episcopal Church**, located at the "V" just beyond Elkin St. The church is a much-photographed beauty whose image is often seen in Gold Country publications. (See the photograph at the front of this book.) Built in 1860, it's considered by many to be the most attractive frame structure in the Mother Lode, and it still serves an active congregation.

Directly across the street from the church is another red beauty, the **Street-Morgan Mansion**. It's a Queen Anne style Victorian built in 1896, and today houses business offices.

Miners from Sonora, Mexico settled here in 1848 (hence the name). After the newly formed California Legislature levied a $20 per month tax on "foreign" miners (about $200 today), some bigoted and greedy "gringos" started stealing the Mexicans' diggings. Although 2,000 Mexicans were forced to leave, some stayed and became outlaws, retaliating with many robberies, beatings and killings attributed to them. We'll tell you about one of those outlaws, Joaquin Murieta, as we drive through Mokelumne Hill this afternoon,

*****

ALTERNATIVE ATTRACTION #2

Toulumne County Museum and History Center

Housed in the former Tuolumne County Jail, which held criminals and rowdies from 1857 to 1960, this museum holds an interesting display of gold and quartz, historic photographs, weapons, tools and wagon parts. Two of the old jail cells display a typical high-country bunkhouse and a gunsmith shop.

Open Sunday through Friday, 10am-4pm and Saturday, 10am-3:30pm; 158 W. Bradford Ave., Sonora 95370; 209-532-1317; *www. tchistory.org.*

*****

Columbia State Historic Park

Now for the centerpiece of our day. (See the photograph at the front of this book.)

From Sonora, continue north on Highway 49 about two miles to Parrot's Ferry Road and follow the brown Columbia State Park signs another two miles to the parking lot. From there, you'll walk into vehicle-free Columbia.

The park never closes; most businesses are open daily 10am to 5pm; 11255 Jackson St., Columbia 95310; 209-588-9128; *www.parks.ca.gov.*

273-acre Columbia State Historic Park, at 2,143 feet above sea level, is the top attraction in the Mother Lode, drawing more than a half million visitors each year. It's devoted to showing what a real Gold Country town of the 1850's looked and felt like. With mostly original buildings, it's the best-preserved town in the Mother Lode. Here, more than anywhere else, you'll experience the authentic atmosphere of California's Gold Rush days.

Assuming you'd like to have lunch before our walking tour, we thought it would be good to point out your restaurant choices now; all are within two blocks of each other. **Columbia House Restaurant**, at the corner of Main and State Streets, serves American fare. It was formerly a saloon established in 1850. The **Jack Douglass Saloon**, at the corner of Main and Fulton Streets, and **Brown's Coffee Shop**, next to Towle & Leavitt at the corner of Main and State Streets, both serve sandwiches. The **City Hotel Restaurant**, on Main Street between State and Jackson, is a bit fancier and serves American and French cuisine. **El Jardin** (Mexican) and **Billy Whiskers** (Italian) sit side-by-side on Parrot's Ferry/Broadway at State Street. **Lickskillet**, just East of Main on State Street, serves American and varied international fare. (See the next map for street locations.)

Following is a brief history of Columbia. It will help prepare you for what you're going to see during the walking tour. We give you a fair amount of detail here, because Columbia provides an outstanding example of what happened throughout the Gold Country.

"Gem of the Southern Mines"

It all started in March 1850 when a five-person prospecting party led by a physician from Maine, Thaddeus Hildreth, spent a rainy night here on the way to known gold diggings. The following morning, after learning from Mexicans that there was gold in the area, John Walker, one of the five, decided to give panning a try while the party's clothes and blankets were drying out. He found "color" in his first pan and each person in the party was soon earning more than $100 per day (as compared with an average wage of $2 per day in the Eastern States).

The word spread rapidly, of course, and within three weeks 6,000 miners had moved into "Hildreth's Diggins" to share the wealth. One of them, a Francis Avent, found $640 in gold his first day, $380 his second day and about $200 per day until the streams dried up in June.

Like Thaddeus Hildreth, most people heading to the gold fields arrived in California by sea. There were two ocean routes: one, 18,000 miles by sea around the tip of South America into San Francisco; the other was much shorter but required crossing Panama or Nicaragua by boat and mule (this was more than 60 years before the Panama Canal). Some Americans traveled to California in wagons via one of two overland routes. Whether by sea or land, the voyage took between four and eight months and was fraught with hazards. Owing to the great number of miners and the fact that the surface gold was quickly mined out, relatively few who made such arduous journeys struck it rich.

And it wasn't only Americans who flocked to the gold fields in California. There were, of course, the Chinese and Mexicans whom we mentioned earlier. Large numbers followed them from England, Ireland, Germany, France, Italy, Chile, the Hawaiian Islands, and Australia. This was, indeed, a worldwide gold rush.

After the streams dried up in June 1850, they stayed that way for six months, until the Sierra snows began melting and the water runoff again filled the streambeds. That long dry period was a problem, of course, because placer mining requires water to wash the dirt from gold.

Since the Columbia Basin had no natural, continually running streams, the miners had to create them. So when the water dried up again in June of 1851, 160 shareholder-miners banded together to form the Toulumne County Water Company. During the following six months, they created 20 miles of ditches and flumes that would carry water from the South Fork of the Stanislaus River to Columbia.

With a steady supply of water, Columbia became a year-round gold camp of bonanza proportions, until the easy gold ran out in about 1861.

Then, pocket mining and hydraulic mining became important means of gold extraction. Gold had accumulated in numerous depressions of the underlying limestone rock, and miners who located those pockets got very rich. Next came a very destructive method called hydraulic mining in which water was forced through hoses under high pressure and used to loosen the soil down to bedrock.

After that, underground hard-rock quartz mining continued but was not very successful, so most of the town's inhabitants drifted away to other diggings.

It's hard to imagine now, but by 1852 Columbia had more than 150 businesses serving its 4,000 to 5,000 residents. They included 30 saloons and restaurants, four hotels, four banks, seven boarding houses, 21 grocery stores, eight carpenter shops, three drug stores, numerous doctor, dentist and legal offices, and many other establishments of all kinds. When families arrived, the town added churches, schools, libraries and theaters.

By 1854, Columbia had grown to be the fifth largest city in California, with between 15,000 and 20,000 inhabitants. That was the year of the first major fire; it was so all-consuming that not one building from that year remains today. Rebuilding began immediately and was finished quickly. A few structures were made of brick.

When a second major fire destroyed 13 city blocks in 1857, only the brick buildings survived. Among them were: Knapp's General Store (the current Information Center/Museum), the Odd Fellows Building, and the D.O. Mills Bank Building. That was all the inhabitants needed to convince them that the second rebuilding should be of brick structures with iron doors and shutters. Half of the buildings you see today date from the late 1850s, the most prominent ones being the Wells Fargo building and the Fallon and City Hotels. The town also purchased pumpers for the two firehouses, and dug cisterns underground to provide a ready source of water to fight future fires.

As for the buildings you'll see shortly, there are four reasons why, today, we're able to enjoy and be educated by this wonderful memorial to the California Gold Rush: First, most of Main Street was rebuilt in 1857 of sturdy, fireproof brick. Second, a small group of original citizens decided to make Columbia their permanent home, thereby preventing significant damage by vandals. Third, movie companies and tourists found Columbia attractive beginning in the 1920's and 1930's, helping to spur a preservation movement. And fourth, the long-term preservation of Columbia was assured when the town became a State Historic Park on July 15, 1945 and the State began to acquire and renovate the buildings.

If you'd like to look more into the history of this once vibrant city, we suggest two books, *Columbia: A History of The Gem of the Southern Mines*, by Bonita M. Cassel, and *Columbia California: On the Gold Dust Trail*, by Elliot H. Koeppel, both of which can be purchased at the Columbia Gazette Office on Washington Street (209-533-1852; *www.columbiagazette.com*).

So what was the "bottom line" of all this gold mining activity? Columbia's miners sifted through every inch of soil at least twice and produced $87 million in gold from two square-miles of earth, equivalent to $2 billion in today's dollars!

Tour the Town

We suggest that you head first to the Information Center-Columbia Museum at the corner of Main and State Sts. Here, you can look over the interesting photos and artifacts, and ask for a copy of the walking tour brochure titled, "Columbia State Historic Park."

In about two hours, Columbia can be enjoyed on either of two levels. You can stroll around town, casually enjoy its ambiance, and explore its 22 shops—as we did during our first visit. Or you can use the walking tour brochure (or this book) and look more deeply at some of the exhibits that have been set up by the State Park for your edification. The locations of the exhibits that we recommend are shown in detail on the walking tour brochure and are approximated on the following map.

Some exhibits have docents. At other exhibits, you'll look through windows and have the opportunity to push speaker buttons to learn more

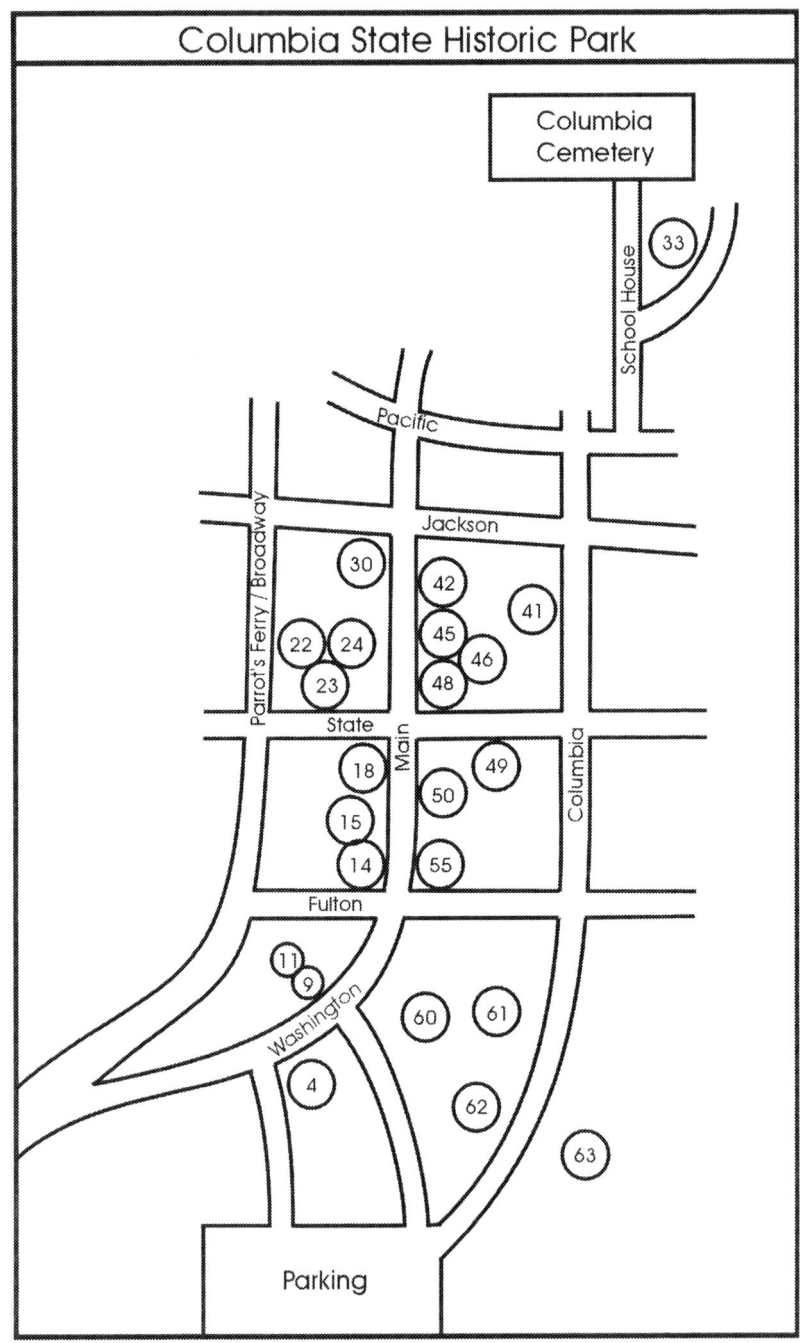

Columbia State Historic Park

about what you see. At still others, you'll walk right in and see things up close. Always, the idea is to give you a feel for what life was like at the height of California's gold mining period. A few sites are not exhibits, per se, but are well worth a look.

Of the 63 sites, we particularly recommend the following:

\# 4 - Columbia Gazette
\# 9 - Wells Fargo Exhibit
\# 11 - Assay Office Exhibit
\# 14 - Jack Douglass Saloon
\# 15 - J.C. Miller Carpenter and Joiner
\# 18 - Justice Court Exhibit
\# 22 - Firehouse Toulumne Engine Company (look for Papeete)
\# 23 - Drug Store Exhibit
\# 24 - Dentist's Office Exhibit
\# 30 - California Store Exhibit
\# 33 - Old Columbia Schoolhouse and Exhibit (and the Columbia Cemetery)
\# 41 - Jail
\# 42 - Firehouse Columbia Engine Company (look for Monumental & Citizen #1)
\# 45 - Butcher Shop Exhibit
\# 46 - Chinese Store Exhibit
\# 48 - Information Center and Museum
\# 49 - Livery Stable Exhibit
\# 50 - Parrott's Blacksmith Shop
\# 55 - Tibbit's House Exhibit
\# 60 - Hidden Treasure Gold Mine Panning (during summer)
\# 61 - Miners Cabin in the Rocks Exhibit
\# 62 - Mining Equipment Exhibit
\# 63 - Columbia Diggin's Tent Town Site

It's Time for a Time Check

By now, it should be about mid-afternoon.

We have not planned another stop on the lovely two-hour drive to Placerville, where we recommend that you have dinner and spend the night. But you may want to consider visiting the Calaveras County Historical Museum Complex in San Andreas (a favorite of ours; see Alternative Attraction #7) and strolling up and down the main street of Sutter Creek (a particularly picturesque town).

Or you may be interested in standing on the very spot where gold was discovered in California, and in seeing a replica of the sawmill that played such an important role in that discovery. If so, read Alternative Attraction #11. Coloma is about 20 minutes' drive beyond Placerville.

A special note for all of you Mark Twain fans: 4.6 miles from where you reenter Highway 49, look for the "Mark Twain Cabin" sign, and the road on your right. The cabin is a replica, but you may find it of interest.

Mark Twain and the Birth of His Famous Frog Story
Now, return to Highway 49 and resume heading north again.

Four and a half miles up the road, you'll pass Jackass Hill on your right. Mark Twain wrote his first short story, *The Celebrated Jumping Frog of Calavaras County* in a cabin on Jackass hill. The story was published in the *New York Saturday Press* on November 18, 1865. It made Twain instantly famous and he went on to write 28 books, becoming the greatest humorist of 19th Century American literature.

The story is about Angels Camp resident Jim Smiley, who trained a frog to jump so he could win bets; but he was one-upped by a stranger who loaded the frog with buckshot when Smiley wasn't looking. No nudge would budge the frog, named Daniel Webster. Smiley discovered the treachery after he'd paid his $40 loss, the stranger had departed, and the buckshot came pouring out when he turned the frog upside down. To commemorate this story and Mark Twain's connection to the area, a jumping frog contest is held every May at the Calaveras County Fair Grounds.

Why Mark Twain wrote *Jumping Frog* on Jackass Hill is also an interesting story...he was hiding from the law!

Born Samuel Langhorne Clemens, Twain grew up in Hannibal, Missouri, became a licensed riverboat pilot on the Mississippi, and moved to the Nevada goldfields at the beginning of the Civil War at age 26. By the way, his pen name is the riverboat pilot's term for water that's two fathoms (12 feet) deep.

Twain worked as a reporter on the *Territorial Enterprise* newspaper in Virginia City, Nevada where he became fast friends with Steve Gillis. While they were together in San Francisco, Gillis conked a bartender on the head during a brawl and was jailed. Twain signed a $500 personal bond and Gillis was released.

Upon learning that the bartender was close to death, Gillis skipped town and returned to Virginia City. Without the funds to pay the $500 bond, Twain also went on the lam, heading to Jackass Hill where Gillis' two brothers were locating and digging pocket mines (rich deposits of gold in gravels or a vein).

During the three months he spent at the Gilles' cabin on Jackass Hill, from late 1864 to early 1865, Twain did no mining, but instead smoked his corn cob pipe and made notes about the people, places and events that he encountered. It was during a visit to Angels Camp, eight miles north, that he heard a story about a frog...and the rest is history.

Twain went on to write such famous works as *Tom Sawyer, Huckleberry Finn, Life on the Mississippi, Prince and the Pauper* and *A Connecticut Yankee in King Arthur's Court.*

Another writer active in the area was Bret Harte, who wrote *The Outcasts of Poker Flat.* Harte's setting, Poker Flat, existed only in his imagination but it was "located" in the general vicinity of O'Byrnes Ferry, about nine miles due southwest of Jackass Hill. Harte worked for a while as a clerk in a Tuttletown store, where Mark Twain was a customer.

About four miles beyond Tuttletown, you'll come to Carson Hill. The historical marker here reports that in 1848 the nearby Morgan Mine produced the largest gold nugget found in the Gold Country. At 195 pounds, it was valued then at $43,000; today it would be worth about $1 million!

Angels Camp

Four miles past Carson Hill, you'll come to **Angels Camp**. At the corner of Main St. and Bird's Way, just beyond where Highway 4 enters Highway 49, you'll see the Angels Hotel on the right, with its green overhanging porch. It was the hotel's proprietor who told Mark Twain the original story that Twain made famous in *Jumping Frog.* Across the street, on your left, is a Jumping Frog monument and an historical marker.

The annual Jumping Frog Jubilee is held at the fairgrounds annually the third week in May. The first contest, in 1928, drew twenty-five frogs and 15,000 spectators!

*****

ALTERNATIVE ATTRACTIONS #3, #4, #5, and #6

Angels Camp Museum

This three-acre museum displays a miniature working stamp mill, miners tools, a labeled rock and mineral display, household items, period clothing, 30 carriages, wagons and carts, two steam engines, a hydraulic monitor, an ore car, a water wheel on its original site, and many other mining period artifacts.

Open daily 10am-3pm, March through December, and Saturday/Sunday, January through February; 753 S. Main St., Angels Camp 95222; 209-736-2963; *www.angelscamp.gov/museum.*

Murphys

An especially quaint and charming town, Murphys is on Highway 4 just eight miles northeast of Angels Camp. One of the town's two founding brothers, John Murphy, at 23 years of age became a millionaire in one year, without mining any gold! He did it by trading with the Miwok Indians, who brought him gold in exchange for blankets and meat. He was just one of many who came to the Gold Country and made their fortunes by supplying the miners.

We suggest that you exit your car and stroll through the town to soak up its ambiance.

Ironstone Vineyards

In our opinion, a visit to Ironstone Vineyards rivals all but a few wineries in the Napa/Sonoma/Alexander Valleys area. The gardens are beautiful, featuring daffodils, tulips, azaleas, and marigolds. Winery tours are available at 11:30, 1:30 and 3:30. (Try the Reserve Chardonnay and Cabernet Franc.) There's an amphitheater that seats 4,000 for outdoor concerts, and an indoor music room for silent movies, weddings and dances. The winery hosts a classic automobile show in the fall; and its tasting room has a gourmet delicatessen. Ironstone also owns and displays a 44-pound gold crystal in its vault. To get there, turn left at the Murphys Hotel, right at the stop sign, and drive one mile.

Open daily 10am-5pm; 1894 Six Mile Road, Murphys 95247; 209-728-1251, *www.ironstonevineyards.com.*

Calaveras Big Trees State Park

Here's another opportunity to see the big trees, if you weren't able to see them in Muir Woods or Yosemite National Park. Drive 16 miles beyond Murphys on Highway 4 and you'll come to **Calaveras Big Trees State Park.** The park has two groves of giant Sequoia trees, a visitor/interpretive center, and seven hiking trails from one-half mile to eight miles in length.

Open daily from sunrise to sunset, but the visitor center is open only from 9am-5pm daily in the summer and only on weekends during the winter; PO Box 120, Arnold 95223; 209-795-3840; *www.bigtrees. org.*

*****

So many things to see, so little time.

After you drive through Angels Camp, continue on Highway 49 for 11 miles to reach San Andreas.

Black Bart: The Gentleman Bandit

San Andreas was the gold camp where the career of Black Bart, California's most famous outlaw, came to an end. He robbed 28 stagecoaches between 1875 and 1883. Wells Fargo had been after him for the full eight years, but he was too clever for them—until he left a clue behind as he hurriedly left his last holdup.

Black Bart had a very interesting *modus operandi*, or "M.O." (in law enforcement jargon):

He always worked alone and on foot—never on a horse—and often on moonlit nights.

He always accosted stages where the horses were slowed on steep hills.

He always wore workman's clothes, a soiled tan duster and a flour sack mask with eyeholes.

Known for his polite manner, Bart wanted only the strongbox and mail sacks.

He never robbed passengers or drivers, and except for one robbery, he stopped only coaches that had no armed guards. His take was smaller—guarded stages carried large gold shipments—but there was less danger of his being shot or captured.

His shotgun was always unloaded and he never injured anyone.

He sometimes left a bit of poetry, signed "Black Bart, the Po8."

The last time was his undoing, because he left behind a handkerchief with a laundry mark that a Wells Fargo detective traced to a laundry in San Francisco. That led to the arrest of one Charles E. Bolton, born as Charles Boles 54 years earlier in rural New York. A Civil War veteran, he had come west to pan for gold, but decided that robbing stagecoaches and enjoying the gentleman's life, the theater, and the best restaurants in San Francisco suited him more.

He pleaded guilty to his last holdup, seven miles southeast of Angels Camp, and was sentenced to six years in San Quentin

Penitentiary. He was released after four years and two months for good behavior, and apparently continued that good behavior, because he was never heard from again.

One intriguing rumor persists: because Wells Fargo no longer wanted to chase Black Bart, the company paid him $125 a month *not* to rob its stagecoaches!

*****

ALTERNATIVE ATTRACTION #7

Calaveras County Historical Museum

We love this museum!

It's here that you can see the jail where Black Bart was held, and the courtroom where he was sentenced. (The courtroom has been updated; the photograph on the wall shows what it looked like in the latter 1800's.) The museum also has an excellent interpretive display on the Miwok Indians, an extensive collection of gold rush artifacts and memorabilia, and a sheriff's office that looks so authentic that you expect the lawman himself to walk in at any moment.

Open daily 10am-4pm; 30 N. Main St., San Andreas 95249; 209-754-4658; *www.calaveralcohistorical.com.*

*****

Joaquin Murieta: Robin Hood or Badman?

Mokelumne Hill, or "Moke Hill" as the locals call it, is eight miles north of San Andreas. Founded in 1848, it grew to 15,000 miners during its Gold Rush heyday. Its most noteworthy building is the restored two-story, circa-1851 Hotel Leger.

We encourage you to drive in and out of this hideaway-looking town—which is apparently what it was. It's reputed to have been the headquarters of Joaquin Murieta, whom we mentioned when we were in Sonora. Thanks to a novel written in 1854 by John Rollin Ridge, *The Life and Adventures of Joaquin Murieta*, he developed a larger-than-life reputation as a handsome, dashing ladies man who had Robin Hood characteristics.

Here's where fact and fiction become considerably blurred. One story has Murieta being driven out of San Andreas by greedy gringo miners. Another is that he was tied to a tree in Murphys where he was beaten, his brother killed, and his wife abused. No matter. He apparently got his revenge on the American miners, living a life of crime for the next few years—until he was captured, and his head put in a jar, pickled, and put on display.

We're certainly not intending to glorify lives of crime—their crimes did *not* pay—but California Gold Country history would be less exciting without Joaquin Murieta and Black Bart, wouldn't it?

Jackson

Six miles farther north on Highway 49, you'll come to several attractions northeast of town that may deserve a look during your next visit to the area. In **Kennedy Wheels City Park**, are two giant wooden wheels used after 1912 as part of a system that transported mine tailings to a reservoir. **Volcano** is a picturesque and particularly well-preserved Gold Rush town that's fun to explore. And, just north of Volcano is **Daffodil Hill**, not a town, but a four-acre hillside that's crammed with thousands of planted daffodils—spectacular to see in late March. Nearby is **Indian Grinding Rock State Historic Park** (see below).

*****

ALTERNATIVE ATTRACTION #8

Indian Grinding Rock State Historic Park

This 135-acre park is dedicated to portraying the Miwok Indian way of life. It features a reconstructed Miwok Indian village, bark houses, a large ceremonial roundhouse, acorn granaries, and the Chaw'se Regional Indian Museum which contains displays of baskets, jewelry, tools and other artifacts. There are also 23 campsites, and two trails, one of which is a half-mile self-guided nature trail. The park's centerpiece is a rock that spreads 7,700 square feet and contains 1,185 mortar holes and 350 two-thousand-year-old petroglyphs. The Miwok used the holes for grinding acorns and seeds into meal to make edible food. This is the largest such rock in North America.

The park is open sunrise to sunset. The museum is open daily 11am-3pm weekdays and 10am-4pm weekends; 14881 Pine Grove-Volcano Rd., Pine Grove 95665; 209-296-7488; *www.parks.ca.gov.*

*****

Sutter Creek to Placerville

Next up is **Sutter Creek**, one of the more comely and best-preserved towns in these foothills. It's a little over four miles north of Jackson. Like Jamestown and Sonora, it has a street full of 1890's brick and stone buildings with overhanging balconies, and is a nice place to take a stroll and browse the antique shops. We'll have more to say on John Sutter, the person for whom the town is named, when we get to Coloma and Sacramento. Leland Stanford—railroad magnate, California state senator, governor and founder of Stanford University in Palo Alto—got his start here when a customer in his store settled a debt with a share of the Lincoln Mine. It paid off handsomely months later when a rich vein was discovered in the mine.

Driving on, we'll pass through: quaint **Amador City** with its antique shops and standout Imperial Hotel; **Drytown**, which got its name because of its dry diggings (Columbia was called "Drytown" for a short while); and **Plymouth,** which is known for its "gold in a bottle."

Europeans who flocked to the gold diggings first planted grapes in this area in 1850. A number of miners turned to commercial wine production in the 1890's after the "easy" gold ran out. Today, there are 40-some wineries in the Sierra foothills, 25 of which are in Amador County where Plymouth is located. Most are small and family-owned. The area is especially well known for its robust Zinfandel wines. Our favorite is produced by Montevina Winery, located just northeast of Plymouth. Montevina is owned by Sutter Home Winery, which we'll visit when we get to the Napa Valley on Day 7.

Placerville

Placerville is 20 miles to the north of Plymouth. This is where we suggest you have dinner and spend the night. Before or after dinner, take a stroll on Main Street where you'll find a 50-foot replica bell tower (which has served as the town's fire alarm since 1856), and a pleasant assortment of galleries, boutiques, and architecturally charming buildings.

Placerville's claims to fame are its earlier name, its omelet, its role in the Gold Rush and its famous mercantilists.

Its original name, "Dry Diggins," was quickly replaced by "Hangtown" after it became the first mining town in the gold country to mete out justice by lynching. And it remained Hangtown until 1954 when it was renamed Placerville. But there's still a vestige of the old reputation hanging around—an effigy strung by a noose above the entrance to the Hangman's Tree Tavern (305 Main St.), the site of the infamous, long-gone Hangtree.

What's that about an omelet? The story is that a miner, who had just struck it rich, burst into a restaurant and asked what the most expensive foods were. When he was told, eggs, oysters and bacon, he exuberantly said, "Fry 'em up." It's known as Hangtown Fry and it's available in Placerville today at Chuck's Restaurant and the Hangtown Grill.

As for Placerville's role in the Gold Rush, some $25 million in placer gold was discovered in the area, but its location is what determined the town's longevity. Hangtown was a convenient entryway for prospectors traveling into the gold country from San Francisco, via Sacramento. Even more important to its economic growth and stability was that the town became the major staging point for supplies shipped over the Sierras after the Comstock Lode was discovered in Nevada in 1859. The Pony Express also passed through here from 1860 to 1861, on the way from Sacramento to Carson City, Nevada and points east.

And then there were the mercantilists. Butcher Philip Armour and wheelwright John Studebaker returned east with savings that allowed them to start a meatpacking empire and an automobile company, respectively. Collis Huntington and Mark Hopkins were able to become railroad magnates after selling vegetables and other supplies to miners. Others who made their early fortunes elsewhere in the Gold Country include Levi Strauss, George Hearst and Domingo Ghirardelli. And, of course, Leland Stanford, whom we mentioned earlier.

It's been said that although few miners got rich, most who supplied them did. With shovels, pickaxes, other basic tools and shirts priced between $20 and $50, a pound of butter, cheese and pork at about $6, a bottle of ale about $8 and a blanket at $100, you can see why the mercantilists chose their profession: it was a lot more of a sure thing, and a lot less back-breaking. The prices were exorbitant for those days, but multiply them by ten or more for some idea of what the miners spent in today's dollars!

One other notable person operated out of Hangtown, but his motive was not profit. "Snowshoe" Thompson was his name and he became famous in the 1850's for carrying 80-pound bags of mail across the Sierra mountains in the dead of winter, to and from Genoa, Nevada—while wearing nine-foot long skis that weighed 25 pounds!

*****

ALTERNATIVE ATTRACTION #9

El Dorado County Historical Museum

"Snowshoe" Thompson's skis are on display at the El Dorado County Historical Museum, which also displays one of John Studebaker's wheelbarrows, a Concord stagecoach, equipment and artifacts from the mining, logging and agricultural industries, as well as historical photographs. Open Wednesday to Saturday, 10am-4pm, and Sunday, 12-4; 104 Placerville Dr., Placerville 95667; 530-621-5865; *www.co.el-dorado.ca.us/museum.*

ALTERNATIVE ATTRACTION #10

Apple Hill

This is a cluster of 40 orchards (and six wineries) that can be accessed along eight miles of Carson Road between Placerville and Cedar Grove. The fall Harvest Festival and spring Apple and Pear Blossom Festival are fun but crowded (one-half million people in the fall!). People come for fresh apples, pears, peaches, cherries, strawberries, and plums, as well as baked pies, strudel, apple cider, apple butter, caramel apples and natural honey. For information, contact Apple Hill Growers at PO Box 494, Camino 95709; 530-644-7692; *www.applehill.com.*

ALTERNATIVE ATTRACTION #11

Coloma and the Marshall Gold Discovery State Historic Park

If you get to Coloma early enough, we recommend that you head directly for the museum, which closes at 4:30 p.m. The rest of the park can easily be seen before sunset when the park closes. The museum and historic buildings are open daily 10-4:30; PO Box 265, Coloma, 95613; 530-622-3470; *www.parks.ca.gov.*

The museum tells the history of the Gold Rush and of the gold discovery in Coloma. It contains interesting exhibits about Marshall and Sutter, as well as mining equipment, horse-drawn vehicles, and household articles and tools.

Then take the half-mile Gold Discovery Loop Trail to see the sawmill replica, the original mill site, the gold discovery site and the Bedrock Mortar, where the local Nisenan Indians ground acorns for their food. Also interesting are the original blacksmith shop, Mormon cabin, Wah Hop store and the Price-Thomas and Papini homes. The

Monument Trail will take you past Marshall's cabin to the gold-discoverer's grave and the hilltop monument that's dedicated to him.

A Brief Recounting of the Gold Discovery

Coloma was the birthplace of the Gold Rush in January 1848, and became the first successful gold camp in the foothills, booming to 4,000 residents by July of that year. Today, the town's population is less than 200, with its historic center now largely encompassed by the 280-acre Marshall Gold Discovery State Historic Park.

The Park carries the name of the man who first discovered gold here, James W. Marshall. But the story of that significant event in history really began when John Sutter partnered with Marshall, a carpenter, to build a water-powered sawmill on the South Fork of the American River. Sutter had obtained approval from the Mexican authorities to establish an agricultural colony in Sacramento (then called "New Helvetia," headquartered at Sutter's Fort which we'll visit on Day Six of this tour) and he needed lumber for his building projects.

So Marshall had traveled about 40 miles from Sacramento to this spot, where he put his Mormon and Indian crew to work. The plan was to saw trees into boards and float them downriver to Sacramento.

Marshall made his discovery here in the tailrace, which is a long channel of water that paralleled the American River and brought waterpower to the sawmill. Four days later, he rode to Sacramento to share the information with Sutter. They agreed to keep it secret until the mill was finished, but Sutter bragged about it to Mexican Comandante Vallejo (whom we'll meet on Day Six), and to the fort's Mormon store manager, Sam Brannan. It was Brannan who spread the word in San Francisco and the Gold Rush was on. Brannan became its first millionaire (without mining any gold!)—after buying up all the picks, shovels, metal pans and boots he could find before spreading the word.

As fate would have it, neither Sutter nor Marshall benefited from the discovery. Sutter's dream colony collapsed with the Gold Rush, and neither he nor Marshall was successful at prospecting for gold. Ironically, Marshall died broke and Sutter nearly so.

Crime and Justice in Coloma

Here is an anecdote about the downside of crime in Coloma:

Mickey Free was among the dishonest opportunists—including cutthroats, gamblers and pimps—who descended on the gold diggings to take advantage of the hard-working miners. But Free was more than a cut below most of them.

He and his two partners murdered some 30 miners for their stashes of gold. They chose mainly Chinese miners who worked isolated claims, viciously killed them and buried their bodies. Sheriff David Buel tracked down the murderers and Mickey Free was the first of the trio to be tried and sentenced to hang for his crimes.

Enter Jerry Craine, who was not involved in Free's crime spree. He was hanged because he loved too much, not because he killed too much. The former schoolteacher, married with children "back East," was infatuated with Susan Newman who was being pressured to marry someone else against her will. Unable to be together, they concocted their double suicide, which went awry when Craine successfully killed his lover but not himself.

Free and Craine were simultaneously executed on October 26, 1855 in front of a crowd of 5,000 to 10,000 people—after Craine gave a 45-minute speech on the wages of sin, and the two men sang a 10-minute duet that Craine had written the night before. Not your typical vigilante hanging depicted in the movies, is it?

*****

It's Dinnertime!

- **Cafe Luna** (a favorite of ours), California cuisine, 451 Main St., Suite 8, Placerville 95667, 530-642-8669, no Web site, $$-$$$.
- **Casa Ramos**, Mexican cuisine, 6840 Greenleaf Dr., Placerville, 530-622-2303, *www.casaramos.net*, $-$$.
- **The Forester Restaurant** (another favorite), American-pub cuisine, 4110 Carson Rd., Camino, 95709, 530-644-1818, *www.foresterrestaurant.com*, $-$$.
- **Johnny D'Carlos**, Italian cuisine, 482 Main St., Placerville 95667, 530-626-1612, $-$$$.
- **Original Mel's Diner**, American cuisine, 232 Main St., Placerville 95667, 530-626-8072, no Web site, $.
- **Powell's Steamer Co.**, Seafood, 425 Main St., Placerville 95667, 530-626-1091, no Web site, $$.
- **Sequoia Restaurant**, American cuisine, 643 Bee St., Placerville 95667, 530-622-5222, *www.sequoiaplacerville.com*, $$-$$$.

Ginnodo-recommended B&Bs/Inns

- **Blair Sugar Pine B&B** - 2985 Clay St., Placerville 95667, 530-626-9006. fax 530-295-9034, *www.blairsugarpine.com,* $$
- **Combellack-Blair House**, 3059 Cedar Ravine, Placerville 95667, 530-622-3764, *www.combeblair.com,* $$.
- **The Coloma Country Inn**, 345 High St., Coloma, 95613, 530-622-6919, *www.colomacountryinn.com,* $$-$$$.
- **Fitzpatrick Winery & Lodge**, 7740 Fair Play Rd., Fair Play, 95684, 800-245-9166, fax 530-620-6838, *www.fitzpatrick winery.com,* $$.
- **Fleming-Jones Homestead B&B** - 3170 Newtown Rd., Placerville 95667, 530-344-0943, *www.robinsnestranch.com,* $$-$$$.
- **GlenMorey Country House**, 801 Morey Dr., Placerville 95667, 530-306-3481, *www.placervillebedandbreakfast.com,* $$.
- **The Seasons Bed & Breakfast** - 2934 Bedford Ave., Placerville 95667, 530-626-4420, *www.theseasons.net,* $$.
- **Albert Shafsky House** - 2942 Coloma St., Placerville, 95667, 530-642-2776, fax 530-642-2109, *www.shafsky.com,* $$.

AAA- or Mobil-Recommended Motels/Hotels

- **Best Western Placerville Inn** - 6850 Greenleaf Dr., Placerville 95667, 800-780-7234, 530-622-9100, fax 530-622-9376, *www.bestwestern.com,* $$.
- **Historic Cary House Hotel** - 300 Main St., Placerville 95667, 530-622-4271, fax 530-622-0696, *www.caryhouse.com,* call for rates.
- **Mother Lode Motel** - 1940 Broadway, Placerville 95667, 530-622-0895, fax 530-344-0159, no Web site-"google" it, $.
- **National 9 Inn** - 1500 Broadway, Placerville 95667, 530-622-3884, no Web site-"google" it, $.

Woodall's-recommended Campgrounds

- **KOA-Placerville**, Placerville; drive 8 mi. W on Hwy 50 from jct. with Hwy 49 to Shingle Springs Dr., then 1/2 mi. W on Rock Barn Rd.; 530-676-2267; *www.koa.com.*
- **American River Resort**, Coloma; drive S 1/2 mi. on Hwy 49 from jct with Lotus Rd. to Coloma Heights Rd. and New River Rd.; 530-622-6700; *www.americanriverresort.com.*

- **Coloma Resort**, Coloma; drive 8 mi. N. from Hwy 50 on Hwy 49, then 200 yds. NE on Mt. Murphy Rd.; 530-621-2267; *www.colomaresort.com.*

Day Five - **Lake Tahoe**

In the middle of this chapter, we outline several alternative activities in the Lake Tahoe area. If you've previously ridden the Heavenly Gondola and the Tahoe Queen, and don't want to repeat them, we hope that you'll find something pleasing among the alternatives.

After a full day of focusing on the history of the Gold Country, you're probably ready for a scenic drive in the Sierras, a ride on the Heavenly Gondola to a panoramic view from nearly 3,000 feet above Lake Tahoe, and a paddlewheel boat ride on Lake Tahoe itself. Then, we point you toward the Tallac Historic Site, where you'll tour an enclave of Gatsby Era summer homes on the lake, and learn about the once-spectacular Tallac Resort. After that, we'll walk through adjoining Taylor Creek, where you'll enjoy views of water, mountains, fish and forest. Finally, we'll drive to Sacramento, and along the way, learn how the transcontinental railroad was built across that formidable barrier called the Sierra Nevada Mountains.

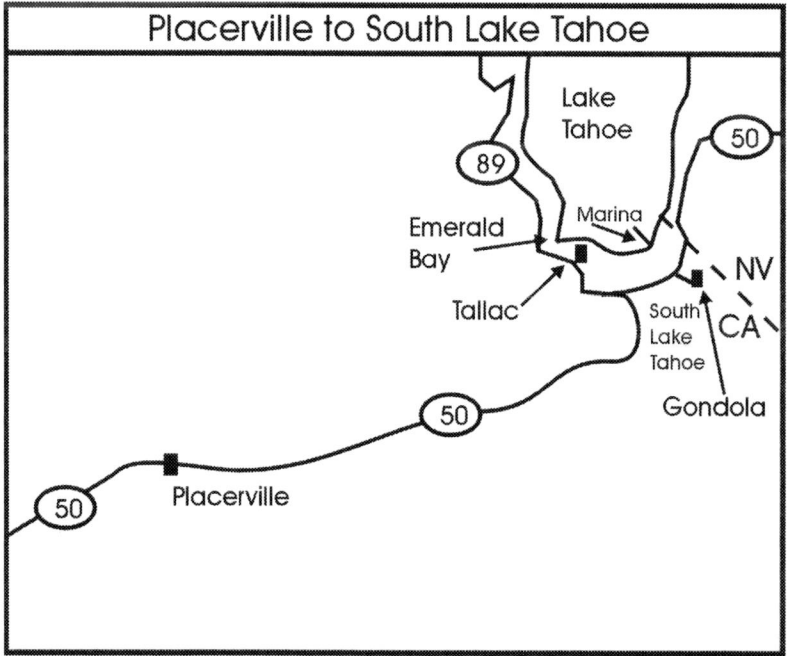

South Lake Tahoe

It will take you about 1-1/4 hours to drive the 57 beautiful miles over the Sierra Nevada between Placerville and South Lake Tahoe. That's a lot quicker than the Pony Express riders as they raced along this route in 1860-1861. (We tell you more about the Pony Express in the next chapter.) It was also a lot quicker than the supply wagons that traveled this route to the gold and silver mines in Virginia City, Nevada in the 1860s and 1870s.

So as you zip along this modern roadway, look about you and try to imagine the historic struggle of express ponies and teams of supply horses as they surmounted this rough mountain country.

As you approach South Lake Tahoe, you'll want to check the hour, and read ahead in this book, to determine whether you'll have enough time to ride the Heavenly Gondola before your paddle wheeler departs.

The **Gondola at Heavenly** is located 4.5 miles from the junction of Highways 50 and 89, or, one-half block west of Stateline. To get to the city-owned parking garage, turn right off Hwy 50 onto Park Ave./Heavenly Village Way, then turn left onto Bellamy Court.

The hours are subject to change, but generally the gondola operates daily 10am-4pm year-round, except for late October through late November when maintenance is performed. You can get the latest schedule information at 1-800-HEAVENLY or *www.skiheavenly.com/resort/summer/gondola.*

Altogether, your two mile/17-minute ride up, your time on the observation deck, and the ride back down will take about 1-1/4 hours. Is it worth the $20+ cost? Emphatically, yes! You'll have a bald eagle's view, from the observation deck at 9,123 feet elevation, which takes in the deep blue lake to the north, the heavily hiked Desolation Wilderness to the west, and Carson Valley in Nevada to the east. This view, from 2,900 feet above the lake, is one that you'll remember for a long time.

As you stand on the observation deck, note that Lake Tahoe, is the largest alpine lake in North America, the second deepest lake in North America, and the tenth deepest in the world.

When explorer John C. Fremont and his guide, Kit Carson, first saw Lake Tahoe in 1844, this was the domain of the Washoe Indians, who called the lake "Da Ow," or "big water." Settlers pronounced it "Tahoe". Later in that same decade, migrating white men and their families saw the lake as they came through the area on their way westward. The ill-fated Donner Party, which we'll learn about later today, was among them.

Statistically, the lake is 22 miles long, 12 miles wide, and has a surface area of 191 square miles. Two-thirds of it is in California, one-third in Nevada. The shoreline drive around the lake is 71 miles long. Tahoe's water, fed by 63 streams, is 99.9 percent pure, and visibility extends to 75 feet below the surface. The lake's depth is so great at its deepest point, 1,645 feet, that its water could cover a flat area the size of California fourteen inches deep—enough to supply everyone in the United States with 50 gallons of water per day for five years! Due to its depth and constant motion, the lake never freezes. And how cold is that water, you ask? It's between 41 and 47 degrees Fahrenheit at 200 feet. Brrrrr!

Lake Tahoe sits 6,226 feet above sea level and the highest mountain in the area is Freel Peak at 10,881 feet. The lake feeds only one drain-off, the Truckee River, which exits at Tahoe City. There is sunshine in the area approximately 274 days a year. The Tahoe Basin experiences 30 inches of precipitation and 18 feet of snow annually. The mountains, lake and snow make this a year-round vacation destination.

Is It Lunchtime?

We have two recommendations. The first is the outdoor **Adventure Peak Grill,** located at the turnaround of the gondola ride, one-half mile beyond the observation deck. If it's a nice day, you'll thoroughly enjoy the mountain ambiance and the grill's sandwiches.

The second is the **Wolfgang Puck Express** at the base of the gondola ride, near the entrance to the parking garage. This restaurant has a nice selection of salads, sandwiches, pastas, specials and pizzas. Note that Wolfgang Puck's will validate your parking ticket, but the gondola and the Adventure Peak Grill will not.

Paddlewheel Boat Ride to Emerald Bay (See the photograph at the front of this book.)

We think of this as a "must" activity, unless the weather is bad. The boat ride is a feast for the eyes and 2-1/4 hours of pure serenity. (However, we haven't taken the 11:30am kid-focused cruise on the Tahoe Queen. It would be fun, but we would probably have to settle for "very pleasant" instead of "serene.")

One company offers cruises to Emerald Bay on two Mississippi River-type paddleboats; one boat is berthed at Ski Run Marina in South Lake Tahoe (the one we recommend) and the other is berthed at Zephyr Cove, on the Nevada side of the lake.

We suggest that you telephone ahead (800-23TAHOE or 530-541-3364) to verify departure times, since they are changed periodically, and also to make reservations (which are advisable during the summer months).

The **M.S. Dixie** operates daily, year-round, from Zephyr Cove, which is three miles north of Stateline on Hwy. 50. (Unfortunately, the drive from the state line to Zephyr Cove is a nearly-continuous strip of casinos, motels, shopping centers, gas stations and restaurants that considerably detracts from the great natural beauty of the area.) Cruises to Emerald Bay depart Zephyr Cove at 11am and 2pm during the summer; boarding begins a half hour before that. From the end of October to mid-April, departures are at 1pm. We have not sailed on this boat, but understand that she has three decks, carries 550 passengers, shows a video titled "The Sunken Treasures of Lake Tahoe," and otherwise the same Emerald Bay experience, food available and pricing as the Tahoe Queen. So, if the Tahoe Queen's schedule doesn't work for you, this paddlewheel boat is a good backup.

It's easy to get to Ski Run Marina and Tahoe Queen from the Heavenly Gondola: just backtrack on Hwy 50 about 3/4 mile and you'll see it on your right.

Tahoe Queen conducts cruises twice daily to Emerald Bay between mid-May and mid-September: at 11:30am (kid-focused and featuring a dinosaur-like character, "Tahoe Tessie," and kid-friendly food); and 2:30pm featuring "Mark Twain" as narrator. Boarding begins a half hour before departure times. From mid-September to the end of October, Emerald Bay cruises depart daily at 12 noon. From November through May, they depart at noon, but only on Saturday and Sunday.

Tahoe Queen is a two-deck, 144-foot long paddlewheeler accommodating up to 500 passengers. Views are fine from the lower (more protected) deck, but you'll want to be on the top deck for the narrated explanation of Emerald Bay. An interesting fact: three glaciers carved their way down the face of the mountains; one broke through to the lake and created Emerald Bay. The other two created Fallen Leaf and Cascade Lakes (out of sight a short distance southeast of Emerald Bay).

You'll see Vikingsholm Castle, a replica of an 11th century 38-room Viking fortress, built in 1929 as a summer residence. It can be reached only by hiking a mile downhill, dropping 500 feet in elevation. Yes, you can tour Vikingsholm during the summer months.

You'll also see the only island on Lake Tahoe, Fanette, which is topped by the ruins of the 16-foot square "Tea House," used by the owners of Vikingsholm to serve afternoon refreshments to guests.

Directly above Vikingsholm is Inspiration Point, where photographers and gawkers alike are indeed inspired by an incredible view of Emerald Bay, and Lake Tahoe beyond. Later, we'll suggest that you stop there for inspiration and photographs. (See the photo at the front of this book.)

Food is available for purchase on board Tahoe Queen, and an interesting video, "Mysteries Beneath Lake Tahoe," is shown on the lower deck.

We're sure you'll find this to be a very beautiful and memorable boat ride.

Tallac-Taylor Creek or the Donner Memorial?

After the paddleboat cruise, you may want to choose between two activities: the Tallac Historic Site and the adjoining Taylor Creek Visitor's Center, or, Donner Memorial State Park. Your choice will be influenced, of course, by which interests you most, and whether you have enough time to get to the Donner Site by about 3pm, since it closes at 4pm.

Tallac and Taylor Creek are nearby; Donner is 40-miles/an hour's drive away. Reading ahead will help you decide.

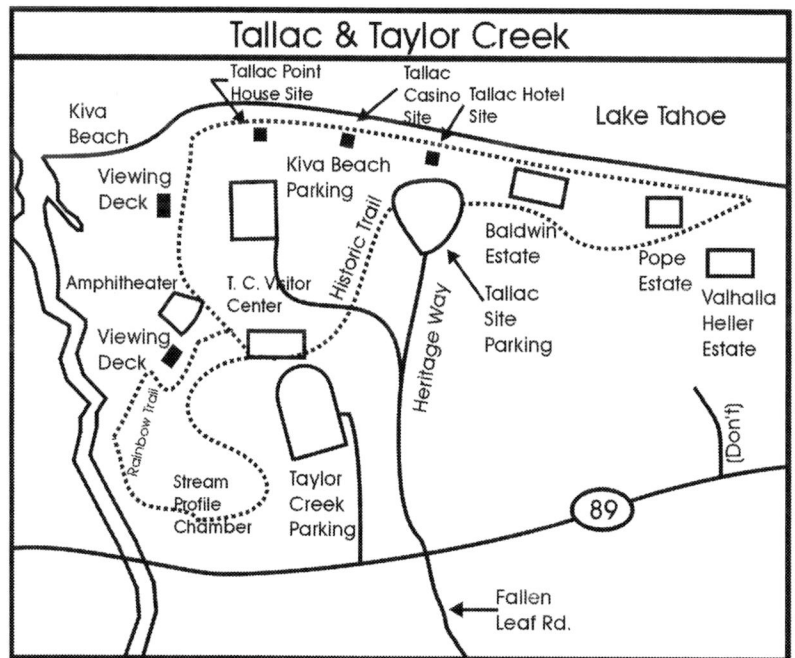

Tallac Historic Site

You can park just once to take in both Tallac and Taylor Creek, which sit side-by-side on the south shore of Lake Tahoe. They are laid-back gems managed by the U.S. Forest Service.

From Ski Run Marina, follow Hwy. 50 west to the junction with Hwy. 89, then drive north about three miles on Hwy. 89 (Emerald Bay Road) to the Tallac Historic Site entrance.

The Tallac Historic Site has two parts to it: 1) three historic homes, and 2) the site of the former Tallac Resort.

Stroll past the three grand historic homes to get a glimpse into opulent Gatsby-era summer living. The homes are side-by-side along the lake, connected by a path that weaves between them. All are shaded by soaring pine trees. The Pope Estate was built in 1894, the Baldwin Estate in 1921, and the Heller Estate (also known as Valhalla) in 1923. The Baldwin Estate has a museum, which is open 10am -4pm, mid-June through mid-September and on weekends the rest of the year; 530-541-5227; *www.tahoeheritage.org.* The museum sells a booklet with photos, titled "Tallac Historic Site." The Pope house can be toured from mid-June through mid-September, at 11am, 1pm and 2:30pm.

On the east side of the Pope Estate, you'll find another path that will take you back toward the parking lot, but you won't be going to the parking lot just yet. We'd like for you to see the site of the Tallac Resort and to enjoy the pleasures of Taylor Creek.

Immediately west of the three mansions there was once an elegant summer resort known as Tallac (sounds like "shellac"). It was built in the 1880s by "Lucky" Baldwin and was *the* place to be on Lake Tahoe until the early 1920's. (If you're wondering, "Lucky" got his money and name as a land developer, stock speculator, and gambler.)

The resort catered mostly to wealthy folks from San Francisco, Sacramento and Virginia City, so the hotel's beautifully appointed dining room had an elaborate gourmet menu of eight-course meals served while a string orchestra provided background music. As one of our sources said, "Lucky had created an atmosphere of 'conspicuous consumption,' and the guests loved it."

Tallac's 3-1/2 story resort hotel once sat immediately north of where the parking lot is now. It had 30 sleeping rooms accommodating up to 100 guests. Farther west, another older hotel, called Tallac Point House, and some cottages, accommodated 150 more guests. All rooms had electricity and steam heat.

Between those two hotels sat the Tallac Casino, also 3-1/2 stories tall, with a ballroom, four bowling alleys, billiard and pool rooms, a stage for theatricals and musical performances, and of course, its gambling facilities. A portion of the casino's foundation is still visible. Elsewhere on the resort's 2,500 acres were a large vegetable garden and 200 milk cows, which helped supply the resort's kitchen.

Since gambling was illegal in California, the casino's promotion as "The Greatest Casino in America" posed an interesting challenge: how do you make it disappear before the law arrives? The answer was: put the casino's grapevine warning system into effect while the sheriff was on his way, so that the gambling equipment could be safely hidden.

Very interesting, too, is how people got here, since they couldn't drive in buggies or automobiles (there were no roads in the area then). Most people used three consecutive conveyances: the Southern Pacific Railroad from San Francisco and Sacramento to Truckee (50 miles north), a stagecoach from Truckee to Tahoe City on the lake, and the steamer *Tahoe* the rest of the way. Once here, guests enjoyed steamer rides, canoeing, sailing, hiking, fishing, horseback riding, casino gambling, ballroom dancing, bowling, lawn tennis, croquet, superb dining, and other resort activities. All this for $32.50 a week, per person—about $700 in today's dollars.

"Lucky" Baldwin's daughter, Anita, had the Tallac Resort torn down in 1927, because she didn't want to bother with the needed rehabilitation and upkeep.

Taylor Creek

Now, let's take a beautiful 1.7-mile walk along the lake and through the woods..."and to grandmother's house we go," with apologies to Little Red Riding Hood.

The trail between the Tallac Hotel and Tallac Point House was known as the Promenade, or Cottage Walk. It had lights mounted on poles, so guests could stroll between the two buildings at night.

After you reach Tallac Point, the trail turns south and you'll enter Taylor Creek on Lake of the Sky Trail. There are two viewing decks along this trail. Both offer beautiful views of the nearby marsh and farther mountains, the tallest of which is Mount Tallac at 9,735 feet elevation.

Adjacent to the Taylor Creek Visitor's Center, you'll find the entrance to Rainbow Trail. You'll walk on a paved path through the marsh and be able to see fish at eye level through a glass cutaway of Taylor Creek known as the Stream Profile Chamber.

The Visitor's Center is run by the U.S. Forest Service, and has a nice selection of area trail maps, guides, post cards and gift items available for purchase. It's open 8am-5:30pm, mid-June through October; 530-543-2674.

The final quarter-mile stretch of your walk will take you along the Tallac Historic Trail, which runs between the Visitor's Center and the Tallac Historic Site parking lot.

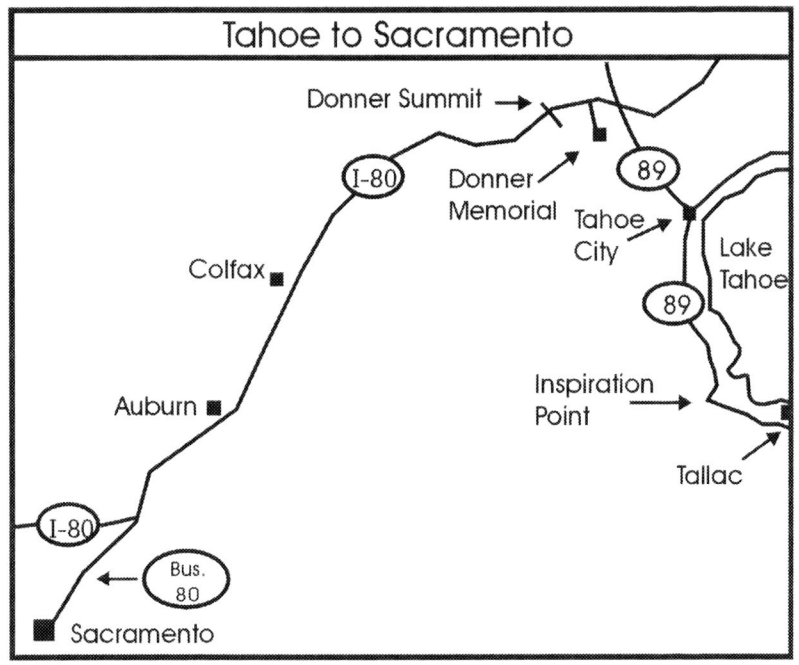

Tallac to Interstate 80

Next, continue north on Hwy. 89 and enjoy the drive along the lakeshore. You'll want to stop at Inspiration Point, four and one-half miles from Tallac, to admire the wonderful view of Emerald Bay. This is one of the most-photographed scenes in California. If the parking lot is full at Inspiration Point, continue north on Highway 89 about a quarter-mile to the parking lot that serves Vikingsholm Castle.

Be sure to follow Hwy. 89 when it leaves the lakeshore at Tahoe City and heads northwest toward I-80.

*****

ALTERNATIVE ACTIVITIES IN THE LAKE TAHOE AREA

As you might guess, the opportunities in this area are almost endless. We've chosen to list here the most popular ones. Contact the South Lake Tahoe Chamber of Commerce (see immediately below) for others.

Hiking

There are many hiking opportunities in the area. Visit or telephone the South Lake Tahoe Chamber of Commerce for trail information. Ask for the pamphlet provided by the US Forest Service that features the 12 most popular trails near the southwest portion of Lake Tahoe. The Chamber is open daily 9am-5pm during the summer and Monday-Friday 9am-5pm during winter; 3066 Lake Tahoe Blvd. (Highway 50), South Lake Tahoe 96150; 530-541-5255; *www.tahoeinfo.com.* Or, you can get the Forest Service trail pamphlet at the Taylor Creek Visitor's Center.

Skiing

Heavenly Valley, Sierra-At-Tahoe and Kirkwood Ski Resorts are all convenient to South Lake Tahoe. (Squaw Valley, site of the 1960 Winter Olympic Games, is about eight miles northwest of Tahoe City.) Cross-country skiing is available at Kirkwood, Hope Valley, and Camp Richardson, which also offer snowshoeing. There are also opportunities for sledding in the area. You can get maps and other assistance from the South Lake Tahoe Chamber of Commerce, as shown above.

Lake Tahoe Historical Society Museum

This small museum is next door to the South Lake Tahoe Chamber of Commerce, at 3058 Lake Tahoe Blvd. (Highway 50), South Lake Tahoe 96150, no Web site. Open Memorial Day through Labor Day, Tuesday through Saturday, 10am-4pm. The museum contains an eclectic collection and photographs on the Washoe Indians, the Pony Express, mining, the railroads, the lake passenger steamers, and the winter sports and gambling industries. Also, there are two historic structures on the grounds.

D.L. Bliss State Park

Two of the hiking opportunities are located in this park: the half-mile-long, brochure-guided Balancing Rock Nature Trail which takes you along the lakeshore; and 4.5-mile Rubicon Trail which traverses the cliffs above the lake. Bliss also features Lester and Calawee Cove Beaches for sunbathing and swimming (brrrr!) as well 168 campsites.

Open mid-May to mid-October; located two miles north of Emerald Bay on Highway 89; 530-525-7277; www.parks.ca.gov.

Vikingsholm

In 1928, wealthy Lora Josephine Knight traveled to Norway, Sweden, Finland, and Denmark with Swedish architect Lennart Palme to gather ideas for her summer residence on Emerald Bay. Of particular interest were wooden churches, stone castles and farmsteads dating back to 1000 to 1500 A.D. What resulted was a lakefront manor—many refer to it as Vikingsholm Castle—built in 1928-29 by 200 workmen. It features round granite boulders and carvings outside, and Nordic fireplaces, paintings on ceilings and walls, intricately carved beams, and Scandinavian antiques inside.

Open daily for half-hour guided tours 10am-4pm from mid-June through August; access is via a steep, one-mile trail from the Vikingsholm parking lot on Highway 89, or via Rubicon Trail from D.L. Bliss State Park; 530-541-3030; *www.vikingsholm.com.*

Gambling

If you have an interest in slots, blackjack, poker, craps or roulette, Stateline, Nevada is the place to find them. You can't miss the casinos, which begin immediately after you cross the California-Nevada state line on Highway 50.

*****

Donner Memorial State Park and Emigrant Trail Museum

After entering I-80 (toward Sacramento), and just past the Agricultural Inspection Station, you'll see the Donner Pass Road exit. It's here that you would turn if you have the time to visit the Donner Memorial.

This site commemorates the harrowing and tragic story of 91 people—eight families and 16 single men—who became snowbound here during the winter of 1846-1847 while on their way from the eastern states to California.

The trouble started way back in Wyoming when the pioneers banded together to take a new "shortcut" through Utah, instead of following the main California Trail through Idaho. The party had to hack out a passable route through the mountains and cross the Great Salt Lake Desert. The result was exhaustion, a three-week delay, and the loss of all their oxen, most of their cattle, several wagons and many possessions.

The Donner Party (named for their elected wagon master, George Donner) arrived here in late October of 1846 and decided to rest before finishing their journey. It was a fateful decision, as, unfortunately, an early heavy snowstorm overtook them, stranding them for the winter.

Although successful at building cabins and shelters to withstand the elements, with only a few cattle to eat, and with deer and fish scarce, they soon began to starve. In December, with the situation desperate, a group of 15 men and women donned snowshoes to hike 100 miles over the summit and down to Sutter's Fort in Sacramento. Thirty-two days later, eight emaciated survivors staggered into a settlement north of Sacramento, having survived on the bodies of those who had died.

It wasn't until February that four successive rescue parties, sent by John Sutter (more on him tomorrow), were able to reach and bring out 35 survivors who had remained behind. By that time, their shelters were buried under 22 feet of snow. That's 22 *feet*, not inches—equivalent to the height of a two-story building! Here, too, there was evidence of cannibalism. Only 49 of the original 91 people survived this dreadful human ordeal.

The video presentation in the Emigrant Trail Museum tells the story of the Donner Party's life-and-death struggle. The museum also contains exhibits about the natural history of the area, the migration of the 1840's pioneers, the transcontinental railroad and the lumbering industry.

Outside, you'll find the Pioneer Monument (dedicated to the 1840's pioneers), the site of two Donner Party cabins, and the starting point of a self-guided nature trail near the museum.

Open daily 9am-4pm, except for the Thanksgiving, Christmas and New Year's holidays; 12593 Donner Pass Road, Truckee, CA 96161; 530-582-7892, *www.parks.ca.gov.*

Building the Transcontinental Railroad

Shortly after you go by the Donner Pass Road exit, you'll crest Donner Summit at 7,239 feet above sea level.

Tomorrow, we'll provide more information about the key people involved in building the transcontinental railroad, but while we're driving along the actual route we thought you'd like learn about what it took to conquer these mountains. It was a most incredible feat, as you'll see. We used as our primary source the fascinating book, *Nothing Like It in the World: The Men Who Built the Transcontinental Railroad 1863-1869,* by Stephen E. Ambrose.

It took five years to build the transcontinental railroad over the Sierras. Today, when it takes about two hours to drive between the Lake Tahoe basin and Sacramento, it's difficult to appreciate the number and magnitude of challenges and hardships endured by those who built it:

Tracks, engines and railroad cars had to be shipped from the East Coast, around the tip of South America, and back up to San Francisco. The mountainous terrain was steep and rose 5,880 feet in elevation. Hundreds of gullies had to be filled, and ravines needed to be spanned by long trestles (railroad grades must be much more gradual than highway grades). Fifteen tunnels had to be blasted out of hard granite. The snowfalls were enormous every winter (more snow falls here than anywhere in the U.S. outside of Alaska). And the Central Pacific had no workforce!

In all history, there had never been an undertaking like it. Its scope was inconceivable to everyone who learned about it—except the engineer who found the route, the four men who financed and managed it, and the mostly-Chinese workforce that they assembled to build it.

Let's give credit where credit is due: the Chinese were the real heroes of this enormous project. Eight thousand left their homeland to labor under arduous conditions for low pay in a foreign country whose language they didn't understand. And they did their work steadily, with great skill, and without complaint. It was the Chinese who filled the gullies, built the trestles, graded the roadbed, cut the trees, made the ties, laid the track, shoveled the snow and, most importantly, bored the tunnels—all in a race with the Union Pacific which was building the railroad westward to their rendezvous.

Tunneling was the most laborious and difficult of all tasks. The Chinese worked in teams of three at the rock face: one holding a rock drill and two swinging heavy sledgehammers to make holes for the blasting powder. Working in three shifts, they were able to tear away only six to twelve *inches* of the granite rock face in a twenty-four hour period. Incredibly slow, but steady, progress was the rule.

The most notorious task performed by the Chinese was blasting a route around the side of a mountain just north of Colfax called "Cape Horn." Hanging in baskets high above the North Fork of the American river, they sculpted a ledge for the roadbed by boring holes with small rock drills and filling the holes with blasting powder. Then after lighting the fuses, they were pulled upward to safety just before the explosions occurred.

And, finally, it was the Chinese who constructed the snow sheds. These were wooden structures—outside tunnels, if you will—that were built to allow trains unimpeded passage during winter. One snow shed was 29 miles long, and during one of the five construction winters was buried under, 65 feet of snow!

(In case you're wondering...Yes, the sparks from the train engines did sometimes set the snow sheds on fire. Eventually, concrete structures replaced the wooden ones.)

So, for the next 60 miles, as you descend from Donner Summit to Auburn, we encourage you to do three things: First, enjoy the spectacular scenery. Second, look for the railroad tracks that weave nearby through these rugged mountains. Third, reflect on the hardships endured by the men who, *with only hand tools*, filled the low places, leveled the high places, built the trestles, laid the roadbed and rails, spiked down the rails, blasted the tunnels, and built the snow sheds during the five long years of surmounting the Sierras. This was a human feat that was incomprehensible then and is hard to imagine even now.

Altogether, the Central Pacific built 154 miles of track within California, and went on to build another 538 miles in Nevada and Utah. Tomorrow, we'll tell you about the completion of the transcontinental railroad.

Arriving in Sacramento

We recommend that you spend the night in downtown Sacramento, so as to be ideally positioned to miss the morning traffic and have a head start on tomorrow's activities.

With that in mind, continue about 24 miles southwest from Auburn on I-80 until you come to the I-80/Business 80 junction. Take the Business 80/Capitol City Freeway six miles to "E" Street or "J" Street, and exit right onto 29th Street. After a few blocks, turn right onto "L" Street and head for your accommodations. (Look to your right at the corner of "L" and 28th Streets and you'll see Sutter's Fort, which we'll visit tomorrow.)

It's Dinnertime!

- **Biba**, Italian cuisine, 2801 Capitol Ave., 916-455-2422, *www.biba-restaurant.com*, $$.
- **Chanterelle**, California cuisine, 1300 H St. in Sterling Hotel, 916-442-0451, *www.sterlinghotel.com*, $$-$$$.

- **Delta King Pilothouse Restaurant**, American cuisine, 1000 Front St., Old Sacramento in the Delta King Riverboat Hotel, 916-441-4440, *www.deltaking.com*, $$-$$$.
- **Ernesto's Mexican Food**, Mexican cuisine, 1901 16th St., 916-441-5850, *www.ernestosmexicanfood.com*, $.
- **Frank Fat's**, Chinese cuisine, 806 L St., 916-442-7092, *www.fatsrestaurants.com*, $$.
- **Joe's Crab Shack**, seafood menu, 1210 Front St., riverfront restaurant in Old Sacramento, 916-553-4249, no Web site-"google" it, $$.
- **Rio City Cafe** (a favorite of ours), California cuisine, 1110 Front St., riverfront restaurant in Old Sacramento, 916-442-8226, *www.riocitycafe.com*, $$-$$$.

Ginnodo-recommended B&Bs/Inns
- **Amber House Bed & Breakfast Inn**, 1315 22nd St., Sacramento 95816, 800-755-6526, 916-444-8085, fax 916-552-6529, *www.amberhouse.com*, $$-$$$.
- **Inn at Parkside Bed & Breakfast**, 2116 6th St., Sacramento 95818, 800-995-7275, 916-658-1818, fax 916-658-1809, *www.innatparkside.com*, $$$.
- **Savoyard Bed & Breakfast**, 3322 H St., Sacramento 95816, 800-7-SAVOYARD, 916-442-6709, no fax, *www.savoyard.com*, $$.
- **The Sterling Hotel**, 1300 H St., Sacramento 95814, 800-365-7660, 916-448-1300, fax 916-448-5066, *www.sterlinghotel.com*, $$$-$$$$.

AAA- or Mobil-recommended Motels/Hotels
- **Best Western Sutter House**, 1100 H St., Sacramento 95814, 916-441-1314, fax 916-441-5961, *www.bestwestern.com*, $-$$.
- **Clarion Hotel Mansion Inn**, 700 16th St., Sacramento 95814, 800-443-0880, 916-444-8000, fax 916-444-9412, *www.sacramentoclarion.com*, $
- **Delta King Riverboat Hotel**, 1000 Front St., Sacramento 95814, 800-825-5464, 916-444-5464, *www.deltaking.com*, $$-$$$.
- **Embassy Suites**, 100 Capitol Mall (on the Sacramento River, adjacent to Old Sacramento), Sacramento 95814, 800-560-7782, 916-326-5000, fax 916-326-5001, *www.embassysuites.com*, $$$.

- **Hartley House Inn**, 700 22nd St., Sacramento 95816, 916-447-7829, fax 916-442-4689, *www.hartleyhouse.com*, $$$.
- **Holiday Inn Capitol Plaza**, 300 J St., Sacramento 95814, 800-288-4595, 916-446-0100, fax 916-446-0117, *www.ichotels group.com*, $$.
- **Hyatt Regency Sacramento**, 1209 L St., Sacramento 95814, 916-443-1234, fax 916-321-3099, *www.sacramento.hyatt.com*, $$$-$$$$.
- **Vagabond Inn Sacramento (Midtown)**, 1313 30th St., Sacramento 95816, 800-522-1555, 916-454-4400, *www.vaga bondinn.com*, $.

Woodall's-recommended Camp Grounds
- **CalExpo RV Park**, Sacramento; drive 3 mi. N on Business I-80 from jct. with Hwy 50, then 1 mi. E on Exposition Blvd. and 1/2 mi. S on Ethan Way; 916-263-3187; *www.calexpo.com*.
- **Sacramento West/Old Town KOA**, West Sacramento; on Lake Rd. at jct. of Interstate 80 and West Capitol Ave.; 916-371-6771; *www.koa.com*.

Day Six - **Sacramento and Sonoma**

Since Sacramento is not a wildly popular tourist destination, as are San Francisco, Monterey-Carmel, Yosemite, Lake Tahoe, and the Gold and Wine Countries, why not just skip Sacramento?

Well, 40 years ago, when we lived in Sacramento, we would have agreed with that. Sacramento has a reputation for being very hot in the summer, and there's not much natural beauty to see. Sacramento is, after all, in the flat Central Valley of California. And 40 years ago, there seemed to be little that tourists would want to see in Sacramento, except that it had an excellent art museum, one of the most beautiful state capitol buildings in the U.S., and historic Sutter's Fort.

Since then, things have changed. And we've become more discerning and more tuned-into Sacramento's historical significance. One fact makes the argument for visiting Sacramento: Old Sacramento State Historic Park draws more than five million people a year.

So, come along with us and let us show you a good time in Sacramento. If you'd rather choose two days in the Wine Country, we provide lots of help in the next chapter.

The logical place to start our day, historically, is at Sutter's Fort and the California State Indian Museum. However, they both open at 10am. Since you can see a fair amount of Old Sacramento State Historic Park by 10 o'clock, we'll begin there and proceed to Sutter's Fort and the Indian Museum after that. Taken together, you'll learn what this gateway to the Sierras looked and felt like during the mid- to late-1800's, about Sacramento's role in opening up the wilderness, and about the Gold Rush, the Pony Express and the transcontinental railroad.

This afternoon, we'll drive to Sonoma and its lovely, historic plaza, where we'll learn how Mexico's Comandante of Alta California dealt with the American uprising called the "Bear Flag Revolt."

If it's summer, you can expect the daytime temperature in Sacramento to be around 100 degrees. But it's a dry heat (low humidity), and if dressed properly you should have a reasonably comfortable day. We lived there for five years and loved the weather, year-around.

Getting to Old Sacramento

Not knowing where you're starting from, we suggest only that you drive west on "L" Street to the corner of "L" and 4th Street. Park in the public garage on your right, immediately after you pass 4th Street, and walk through the "tunnel" under Interstate 5 and up into Old Sacramento.

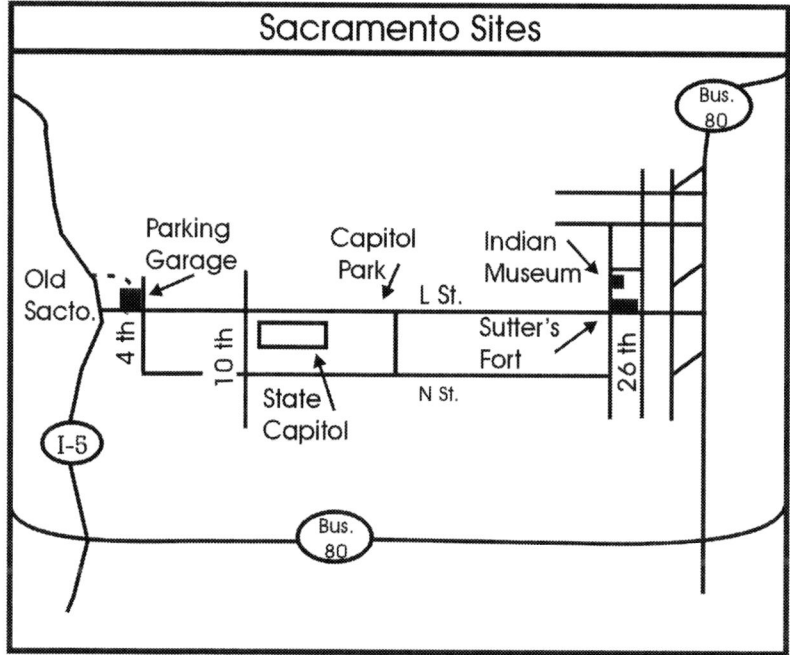

Sacramento Sites

Old Sacramento State Historic Park

As you come up out of the tunnel, you might think, "This place is just a manufactured theme park." But it's not; *it's the real thing.* This was the center of California's commerce during the height of the Gold Rush.

This was the main supply center for the Gold Rush. It was the western end of the Pony Express. And it was where the Central Pacific began building its half of the transcontinental railroad. You'll see evidence of all three as you tour Old Sacramento.

But the evidence nearly disappeared in the 1960s, when these historic buildings were marked for demolition so Interstate 5 could be constructed. Fortunately, history lovers and preservationists came to the rescue, and Interstate 5 was re-routed around the buildings, and other historically significant buildings were moved here onto vacant lots.

According to William M. Holden, whom we cite later, "Old Sacramento is the biggest restoration in the western hemisphere. Some

100 buildings from the 1849-76 epoch have been rebuilt or restored to their Gold Rush-era semblance."

So what you'll see is the heart of early Sacramento, now a 28-acre National Historic Landmark and a State Historic Park, graced with cobblestone streets, gas lamps and wooden sidewalks. In these buildings were housed the hotels, saloons, bathhouses, general stores, places of entertainment, firehouses, butcher shops and many other businesses that served the gold miners and helped jump-start the State of California.

By the way, Sacramento became the capital of California in 1854.

Great Sources

As in the last chapter, our source for this chapter's information on the transcontinental railroad is Stephen Ambrose's book, *Nothing Like It in the World: The Men Who Built the Transcontinental Railroad 1863-1869.*

The other major source of the historical information that you'll be reading here is William M. Holden's book, *Sacramento*, published by Two Rivers Publishing Company. This is a wonderfully complete and well-written book that received the California Historical Society award. It's a great read if you have further interest. It can be purchased at the Visitor Center or Discovery Museum here in Old Sacramento.

Walking Tour of Old Sacramento

With that as general background, let's take a stroll around this looks-like-a-theme-park-but-isn't complex of historic buildings. The numbers in the following map correspond with the sites that we'll pay particular attention to during our walk.

[1]   As you come out of the tunnel, turn right and cross the street.

[2]   Normally, the first stop would be the **Visitor Center** in the B.F. Hastings Building, at the corner of 2nd and "J" Streets, to look at the displays in the adjoining museum and ask any questions you may have. Since the Visitor Center doesn't open until 10:00 am, you may wish to stop here just before you leave Old Sacramento, instead.

The Visitor's Center is open daily 10am-5pm, except Thanksgiving, Christmas and New Year's Days; 1002 2nd Street, Sacramento 95814; 916-442-7644; *www.OldSacramento.com.*

The **B.F. Hastings Building**, built in 1852, is historically significant because it was: 1) the western headquarters of the Pony Express, 2) the Sacramento office of Wells Fargo, 3) the site of the first message sent across the country's transcontinental telegraph, 4) the

office of Central Pacific engineer Theodore Judah, and 5) home of the
State Supreme Court.

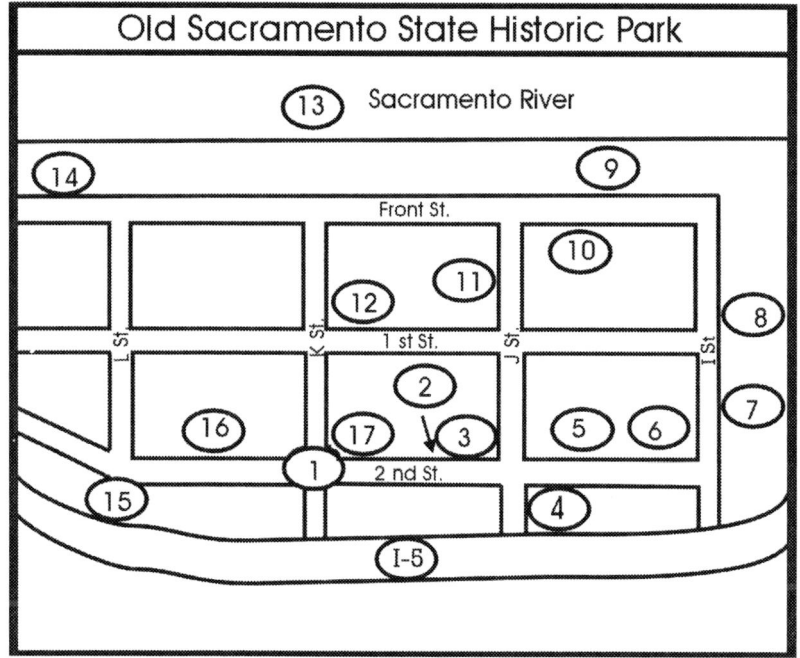

Old Sacramento State Historic Park

[3] Next door, on the corner but still in the B.F. Hastings Building, is
the **Wells Fargo History Museum**. This is the original location of the
company's Sacramento office. Today, it contains a beautifully restored
Concord stagecoach, exhibits on the Pony Express and stagecoach
travel, and Gold Rush artifacts, including gold scales and a telegraph.

[4] Cross the street diagonally to the **Pony Express Monument**, which
was sculpted by Thomas Holland and dedicated in 1976. One can
imagine the horse and rider coming alive in 1860 and taking off toward
Placerville and points East. (See the photograph at the front of this
book.)

   The **Pony Express** was a relay of 500 horses and 121 riders that
carried the U.S. mail in both directions between Sacramento and St.
Joseph, Missouri from April 3, 1860 to late October 1861. The riders,
including a youthful "Buffalo Bill" Cody, changed horses at 157
stations positioned about 10 to 15 miles apart along the nearly 2,000-
mile route, taking about 10 days to complete the run. This important

mail link between East and West ended four days after the transcontinental telegraph was completed. Amazingly, the Pony Express lost only one pouch during its 18 months of operation, despite danger from Indians, harsh weather and mountains.

[5]   Now, cross 2nd Street and walk almost to the corner of 2nd and I Streets. The second building from the corner is the Schroth Building (1854) that housed the **Eureka Baths.** Imagine this: You've just returned to Sacramento after three month's work in the goldfields and you need a bath. The only place to get one is at a public bath, such as this one. The bath water is changed after every 10 bathers. Would you pay extra to be number one?

[6]   Going two lots beyond the Schroth Building, on the corner, you'll find a **sunken courtyard** that is actually the original level of the city's streets. Sacramento's earliest business establishments were often flooded during the spring when the Sierra snows melted and the Sacramento River overflowed its banks. Levees were built along the waterfront, but they didn't work well enough to stop the flooding.

The solution was to raise the streets more than 12 feet, using dirt, gravel and sand dredged from the Sacramento River. Amazingly, it was done with simple tools such as picks, shovels, wheelbarrows and one-horse dump carts. On top of that, building owners needed to either convert first floors to basements and second floors to stores, or jack up entire buildings! More than 200 buildings were raised using jackscrews (similar to old auto jacks), and streets needed to be paved with cobblestones or macadam from Front Street to 29th Street. This gargantuan task took 10 years and was mostly complete by 1873.

Next is the California State Railroad Museum. But before we enter, let's pause to learn the rest of the transcontinental railroad story, which along with what we learned while driving between Donner Summit and Auburn on Day 5, will help prepare you for what you'll see in the museum.

Movers and Shakers of the Transcontinental Railroad

In his beautifully written book, *Nothing Like It in the World: The Men Who Built the Transcontinental Railroad 1862-1869,* Stephen E. Ambrose reveals that the key people in building the Central Pacific Railroad were Theodore D. Judah, the "Big Four" and the Chinese laborers. We've already shared with you some of the heroics of the Chinese. Now we'll tell you briefly about the others.

An experienced railroad engineer in the East, Theodore Judah came to California at just 28 years of age to find the route, raise the money and oversee the building of the Central Pacific's portion of the transcontinental railroad. (The Central Pacific built eastward from Sacramento, while the Union Pacific built westward from Omaha. The two railroads would lay more than 2,000 miles of track and join north of the Great Salt Lake, at Promontory Summit, Utah, on May 8, 1869. Thereafter, a cross-country trip that once took five to six months could be completed in a week.)

It was Theodore Judah and his wife, Anna, who persuaded the U.S. Congress and President Lincoln to authorize and fund the railroad. It was he who found the ideal route over one of the world's toughest mountain ranges. It was he who recruited the "Big Four" to raise the up-front money that was needed to get started.

Unfortunately, Judah did not get to finish the job, or even to see the first rail laid. He contracted yellow fever in Panama and died at 37 years of age following the last of six sea voyages between Sacramento and Washington DC.

But the men he had recruited were up to the task of building the railroad. All four had accumulated modest wealth from their stores in the gold country and Sacramento. All were willing to risk that wealth and apply considerable energy to the building of the railroad. None had prior experience in such an endeavor.

The "Big Four" were: Collis Huntington, who was in charge of finance, borrowed the needed funds in Washington, New York and Boston, and purchased and shipped the engines, cars, rails and supplies to California; Charles Crocker, who was in charge of construction; Leland Stanford, who was President of the Central Pacific and chief politician, and was at the same time Governor of California; and Mark Hopkins, who handled the finances and records.

All four men remained involved in railroading and became extraordinarily rich. Huntington ran the Southern Pacific after it was consolidated with the Central Pacific in 1884; Huntington Beach, California is named for him. Crocker remained in charge of Southern Pacific's construction operations. Stanford became a U.S. Senator and founded Stanford University. The Mark Hopkins Hotel in San Francisco was named for...guess whom?

When you again walk through the tunnel as you return to your car, look for the large mural of the Big Four and Theodore Judah on the right-hand wall.

[7]   The California State Railroad Museum. Located across "I" Street from the sunken courtyard, this museum is widely regarded as the finest railroad museum in North America. Even if you have little interest in railroads, this museum is guaranteed to be stimulating.

Actually, the Railroad Museum is a complex of buildings comprised of: this large building which we'll tour first; the Big Four Building next door (also known as the Huntington & Hopkins Hardware Store); the Central Pacific Railroad Passenger Station around the corner; the Eagle Theater; and the Central Pacific Freight Depot. One ticket will give you same-day access to all five buildings. The Museum also operates the Railtown 1897 State Historic Park in Jamestown, California.

We would normally recommend that you view the museum's fine 20-minute interpretive film, but if you're on our seven-day tour timetable your time will be better spent seeing the rest of the museum complex.

The highlights of this building are: the Sierra Scene with the Gov. Stanford locomotive and snow shed display; the C.P. Huntington locomotive; the dining, post office, Pullman and sleeping cars which you can step aboard; and the outdoor turntable. Altogether, there are 21 beautifully restored locomotives and railroad cars in the museum.

Open daily 10am-5pm, except Thanksgiving, Christmas and New Year's Days; 111 "I" Street, Sacramento 95814; 916-445-6645; *www.californiastaterailroadmuseum.org.*

[8]   Now, continue the walking tour, next door, at the **Huntington & Hopkins Hardware Store**. You'll recognize the names: these two businessmen founded the store in the early 1860's. It's also the building where the meeting was held with Theodore Judah that started the Central Pacific Railroad. But it's not the actual *land* location, because this building was relocated to Old Sacramento when it was scheduled for demolition in the 1960s. Take a look inside at the typical 19th century tools and household items on display.

The second floor of the store houses the reference library of the California State Railroad Museum, which is open from 1-5pm Tuesday through Saturday.

The attached **Pacific Railroad Building** next door, also relocated, housed the offices of the Central Pacific Railroad until 1872, when the railroad's headquarters was moved to San Francisco.

[9]   Central Pacific Railroad Passenger Station. An accurate replica of the original, this building allows you to experience what it must have been like to purchase tickets, to kill time in the circa-1876 waiting rooms (one for men, one for women and children), and then to board the train in the covered track area at this western terminus of the transcontinental railroad.

[10]   Like the passenger station, the **Eagle Theater** is also a replica. A flood destroyed the original miner's theater in 1850. Locals claim that this is California's first theater (it opened in 1849), but you and we know that the First Theater in Monterey has a better claim because it opened two years earlier, in 1847.

[11]   Brannan Buildings. You'll remember our telling you about California's first millionaire, Sam Brannan, when we were in the Gold Country. It was he who bought up all the mining equipment he could, then spread the word about Marshall's discovery of gold. This store carried everything a miner might need—for a price.

[12]   Lady Adams Building. This is the oldest building in Sacramento, the only one originally constructed of brick—which allowed it to survive the fire of 1852. That was Sacramento's first and biggest fire, destroying 40 square blocks, or nine-tenths of the city. What building material do you suppose businesses used during the post-fire reconstruction?

[13]   Waterfront. Up the Sacramento River from San Francisco, in a variety of riverboats, came many thousands of gold-seeking forty-niners and the supplies that they needed. Later, through this waterfront, came the flood of engines, rails, ties, equipment and workers that were required to build the transcontinental railroad. Here, you'll also see the **Delta King**, a restored 285-foot riverboat that operated more recently (from 1927 to 1941) between San Francisco and Sacramento. Today, it's a floating hotel with 44 staterooms, a restaurant, and a theater.

[14]   Old School House. This is not an original structure, but a reproduction of the city's first schoolhouse built in the 1850s. Nevertheless, even a brief look inside will give you a good feel for what school life was like for children of that era.

How About an Early Lunch?

You have three good choices, two of which are very near the Old School House. We enjoyed the food and ambiance at both **Joe's Crab House** (seafood, sandwiches, salads; 916-553-4249), and the **Rio City Cafe** (varied California cuisine; 916-442-8226). Both have indoor and outside seating overlooking the Sacramento River. The third restaurant, **The Firehouse** (California cuisine; 916-442-4772) we know only from recommendations by others. This restaurant is located on 2nd Street between L and K Streets (the next to last stop on our walking tour). The Firehouse is pricey, but according to our survey of exiting patrons, the ambiance is elegant and the food excellent.

As you pay for your lunch, we suggest that you increase your supply of quarters to eight or ten. That's the number that you're likely to need when meter-parking at Sutter's Fort.

There are three more must-see stops on our Old Sacramento walking tour.

[15]   The Theodore Judah Monument is located at L and 2nd Streets, a memorial to the engineer who planned the route of the transcontinental railroad over the Sierra Nevada Mountains.

[16]   The Firehouse. Built in 1853, this was the home of Engine Company No. 3 and is the oldest surviving firehouse in Sacramento. It has operated as a fine restaurant since 1960.

[17]   The Union Hotel. Also built in 1853, this hotel was the departure point for stagecoaches to the goldfields. Imagine the confusion of 24 four-horse stagecoaches assembled in the streets at daybreak, all headed for different places. The California Stage Co., the largest and richest stage company in the world, owned all coaches.

The Drive to Sutter's Fort (and a "Head's-up" about Parking)

After exiting the parking garage at Old Sacramento, drive east on "N" Street. Beginning at 10th and "N," you'll see palm-tree-lined Capitol Park and the circa-1874 State Capitol building on your left. The park consists of 40 acres of lawns, gardens, flowering shrubs and trees from all parts of the world. The Capitol building is a working museum that you should visit if you have time (see "Alternative Attractions" later in this chapter).

When you get to 26th and "N" Streets, turn left and drive two blocks to find Sutter's Fort diagonally on your right.

There are no parking lots in the immediate vicinity of the fort, so your only option is to use the street parking meters. We suggest that you have eight or more quarters with you for the meters. (We didn't have enough quarters, so we were presented with a $25.00 parking violation.) You're likely to spend an hour in the Fort and 30-45 minutes in the Indian Museum.

Sutter's Fort State Historic Park (See the photograph at the front of this book.)

Swiss-born John Sutter was an adventurer and entrepreneur. After fleeing creditors and the law in Switzerland at the age of 31, he spent the next five years working on wagon trains on the Santa Fe and Oregon Trails, driving wild mustangs to Missouri, and traveling to California via the Sandwich Islands (Hawaii) and Alaska.

Sutter arrived in California in 1839. Two years later, he received a land grant of nearly 48,000 acres (about 75 square miles) of wilderness from the Mexican governor of Alta (upper) California. In return, he needed to become a citizen of Mexico and secure the land (tame the Indians) for his adopted country. By 1847, his colony, called "New Helvetia" (New Switzerland), was firmly under way and owned some 2,000 horses and mules, 12,000 cattle, 1,000 hogs and 10,000 sheep. And Sutter was raising about 40,000 bushels of wheat a year. He had gained control of the largely peaceful local Indians as his labor force, and was widely known for being generous to travelers and incoming pioneers. Also in 1847, he sent out the party that rescued the 49 survivors of the Donner Party.

It was Sutter, as you'll remember, who contracted with James W. Marshall to build a water-powered sawmill 40 miles to the east on the south fork of the American River to provide lumber for his building projects. However, Sutter lost most of his skilled, non-Indian workers to gold fever, the mill was never finished, and the projects were never built. And then he lost New Helvetia to squatters and swindlers. Although a pioneer in irrigation, wheat farming, lumbering and blanket manufacturing, he was not a successful businessman; nor was he thrifty or a teetotaler. Sutter died in June of 1880 in Washington, D.C. while trying to obtain reimbursement from the government for his losses.

As for Sutter's Fort itself, you'll see mostly a reconstruction based upon an 1848 map. A similar map will be provided to you as you enter the fort. Proceeding counter-clockwise, you'll first be introduced to John Sutter and his colony. Then, at most doorways, you'll hear audio explanations describing the use of various rooms: barrel-maker's shop, blanket factory (gold-discoverer James Marshall made the looms and spinning wheels), bakery, offices of Sutter and his clerk, kitchen that served 150-200 people per day, carpenter's shop, guest quarters, gunsmith shop, blacksmith shop, candle shop, and trader store. Many artifacts are on display throughout the fort, including: miner's scales, guns, shovels, picks, cooking implements and miner's tools.

Open daily 10am-5pm, except Thanksgiving, Christmas and New Year's; 2701 L Street, Sacramento 95816; 916-445-4422; *www.parks. ca.gov.*

California State Indian Museum

You'll find this gem of a museum immediately behind Sutter's Fort. And you'll find it difficult to tear yourself away once you start perusing its outstanding exhibits.

As a "downer," you'll learn that of about 150,000 Indians in California at the start of the Gold Rush, only 20,000 survived ten years later. Many were killed by miners or died of starvation, and some were enslaved, but most died from epidemics of smallpox, malaria, typhoid fever, cholera and tuberculosis spread by the miners or government-supplied blankets. A poignant story is told about Ishi, the last survivor of the Yahi tribe.

As an "upper," this museum celebrates the native California Indian way of life, with many photographs and artifacts featuring the Miwok, Modoc, Shasta, Paiute, Maidu and many other tribes. These were hunting-gathering-fishing peoples, who spoke 120 different languages, and made beautiful baskets, ceremonial clothing and necklaces. They lived in permanent structures, sang songs accompanied by flutes, and made flour from acorns and blankets from rabbit fur (a large one is on display). Also prominently on display is a dugout canoe.

Open daily 10am-5pm, except Thanksgiving, Christmas and New Year's; 2618 K Street, Sacramento 95816; 916-324-0971; *www.parks. ca.gov.*

*****

ALTERNATIVE ATTRACTIONS IN SACRAMENTO

Three additional attractions are definitely worth your while, if you have the time: the Crocker Art Museum, the Leland Stanford Mansion, and the State Capitol.

Crocker Art Museum

The first and oldest art museum west of the Mississippi River, it's housed in a large, architecturally impressive Victorian mansion and gallery built by Judge Edwin B. Crocker in 1873 for his private art collection. Judge Crocker, older brother to Charles Crocker of "Big Four" railroad fame, served as legal council for the Central Pacific Railroad. The museum's collection consists of European, Californian and Asian artwork, including Old Master prints and drawings. The collection, along with the buildings and grounds, was given in 1885 by Crocker's widow, Margaret, to the City of Sacramento and California Museum Association.

Open Tuesday-Sunday 10am-5pm and Thursday 10am-9pm; 216 O Street 95814; 916-264-5423; *www.crockerartmuseum.org.*

Leland Stanford Mansion State Historic Park

In 1871-72, Leland and Jane Stanford expanded their two-story, 4,000 square foot home to a grand four-story, 19,000 square foot mansion. By then, Leland had served as president of the Central Pacific Railroad (he was also one of the "Big Four") and as Governor of the State of California. He later endowed Stanford University in honor of his son who had died at age 16.

Today, the mansion has an official role in California state government: it is the State's official reception center where dignitaries are welcomed to the State. (The Governor's Mansion would normally serve this function, but has not been used as the governor's residence since Ronald Reagan chose to live elsewhere.) A major makeover, completed in 2005, restored the mansion to circa-1872 condition; 65 percent of the interior detail and furnishings are original, with the rest reproduced from historic photographs. Tours are available daily from 10am-4pm, except during dignitary receptions and Legislative sessions when the tour schedule is more limited.

Open daily 10am-4pm, except Thanksgiving, Christmas and New Year's Day; 800 N Street, Sacramento 95814; 916-324-0575; *www. lelandstanfordmansion.org.*

The State Capitol and Capitol Park

Located at 10th Street and Capitol Avenue, the State Capitol is where the legislature legislates, the Governor governs, and the California State Capitol Museum educates. (Leland Stanford, Ronald Reagan, and Arnold Schwarzenegger are the most famous of the state's governors.) Modeled after the U.S. Capitol in Washington, D.C., the building has a beautiful dome capping a 12-story-high Rotunda inside, as well as marble mosaic floors, crystal chandeliers and lots of polished wood. It was built between 1860 and 1874 for $2.5 million, and restored between 1976 and 1982 for $67.8 million—thereby qualifying as the most expensive restoration, ever, of a state capitol in the U.S. Display rooms include the circa-1906 Governor's and Treasurer's Offices, and exhibits show the scenic, recreational and commercial resources in each of the state's 58 counties. Free one-hour guided tours are conducted daily on the hour from 9am to 4pm. Monday through Friday, go to the Tour Office in the basement (Room B27; 916-324-0333); Saturday and Sunday go to the first floor Rotunda.

Capitol Park provides a most gorgeous setting for the State Capitol building. Sacramento is known as the "City of Trees"—approximately 1-1/2 million of them give the city the look of a forest—and at the heart of that forest is Capital Park, where 450 tree varieties from around the world have been planted in its 40 acres since 1870. Such diversity of trees is made possible by Sacramento's temperate climate. One grove contains trees from famous Civil War battlefields. You can't miss Capitol Park—bordered by L and N Streets and 10th and 15th streets—because it's completely rimmed by towering California fan palms and the State Capitol dominates its interior. Besides the trees, there are many varieties of camellias (which bloom in February and March), grassy lawns and a trout pond. A pamphlet showing the layout of the grounds can be picked up in the Capitol's Room B27 Tour Office or in the Rotunda.

*****

From Sacramento to Sonoma: Mexico's Northernmost Outpost

From Sutter's Fort, drive east a block or two to 29th Street (but don't go under the freeway). Turn right (south) on 29th, drive a couple of blocks keeping to the left, and enter the on-ramp of the Business 80 freeway heading toward San Francisco. Then follow the signs for Business 80 West until the freeway becomes I-80 West. From there, it's about 40 miles to the Highway 12/Napa exit. Follow Highway 12 west for 22 miles (past Napa) into Sonoma's plaza.

We suggest that you visit the Vallejo Home before stopping in the plaza, because it closes at 5:00 pm.

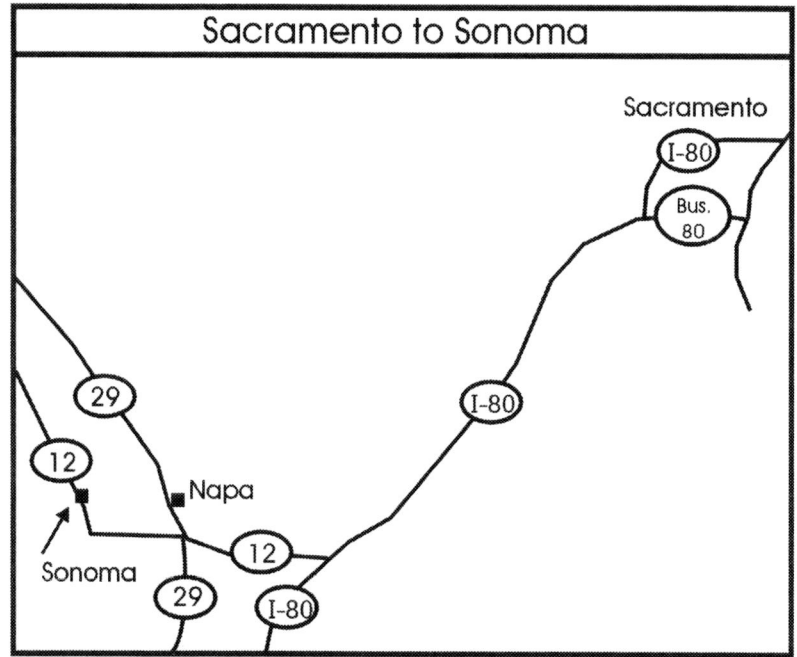

With that in mind, drive around the right side of the plaza, turn left at the top of the plaza onto Spain Street, and drive west three-tenths of a mile to the entrance of General Vallejo's home, on your right.

The Vallejo Home

This home belonged to Mariano Guadalupe Vallejo, Comandante of the frontier region of Alta California at the time of the "Bear Flag Revolt," and namesake of the city of Vallejo. We'll tell you more about the "Bear Flag Revolt" when we return to Sonoma Plaza.

Although everyone called Vallejo "general," he was never technically a general in the Mexican army. His highest rank was Lieutenant Colonel, but we'll go along with the crowd and call him "general."

General Vallejo called his home Lachryma Montis (Latin for "mountain tear"). It was built in 1851-52, some five years after the "Bear Flag Revolt." Interestingly, the house was pre-fabricated on the East Coast and shipped around Cape Horn in sections. As it was assembled onsite, bricks were laid within the walls to help insulate the home.

Vallejo lived here with his wife, Francisca, until his death in 1890 at age 82. The Vallejo's had 16 children, 10 of whom lived to adulthood. In 1933, his daughter, Luisa, sold Lachryma Montis to the State of California to be preserved as an historic site. Today, it's part of the Sonoma State Historic Park.

During your tour of this two-story, five-bedroom Victorian home, you'll see a concert-grand piano, furniture, and many personal items that were owned by the Vallejos. Also on the property are a cookhouse, two small cabins, a spring-fed reservoir, and the Chalet building, which serves as the interpretive center and museum for the home.

Open daily 10am-5pm, except Thanksgiving, Christmas and New Year's Day; Spain St. and 3rd St. W., Sonoma; 707-938-9559; *www.parks.ca.gov.*

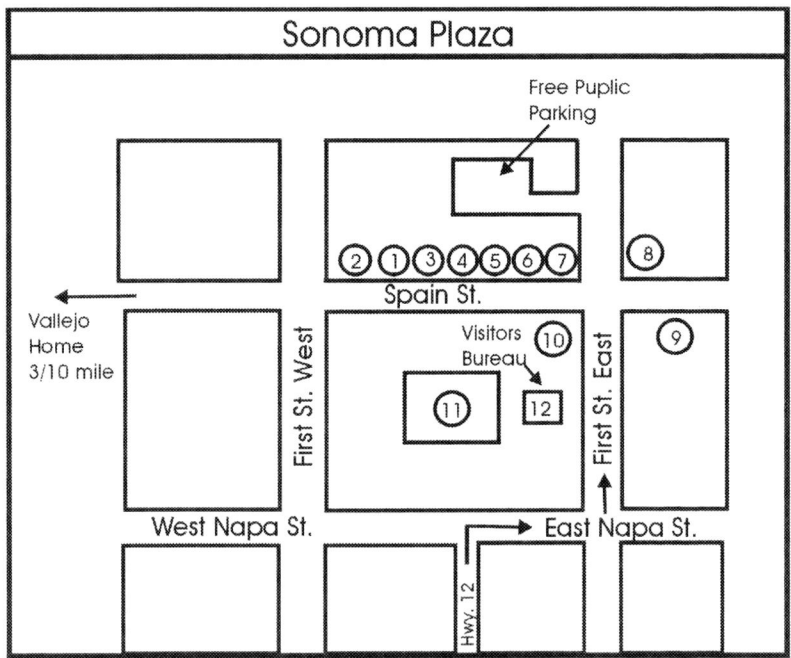

Sonoma Plaza and the "Bear Flag Revolt"

Now return to Sonoma Plaza by exiting left onto Spain Street, and then continue on Spain to First St. East, where you'll turn left, and immediately left again into the parking lot. Then walk between the historic buildings to Spain Street.

As you stand on the sidewalk, try to imagine what Sonoma Plaza looked like in 1846: eight treeless acres and no city hall there in the center of the plaza. The dusty square was criss-crossed by paths and was the place for the garrison's 40 Mexican cavalrymen and 100 Indian soldiers to drill. Livestock grazed here and the area was used for horse races.

The plaza had been laid out by General Vallejo—using a compass and a very long string—when he arrived here in 1835. On its perimeter were mostly one-story adobe homes, occupied by predominantly Mexican families. It was, and remains, the largest plaza of its kind in California.

Most of the structures that you see today around the plaza were built between the late 1850's and the early 1900's. Those that were here in 1846 are shown on the above map: the Swiss Hotel, the Casa Grande with its Indian Servants' Quarters, the saloon atop the Hotel Annex, the Barracks, the Mission, and The Blue Wing. We'll walk by all of them shortly.

Into this scene on the morning of June 14, 1846 came a rag-tag group of 33 Americans, led by a rough character by the name of Ezekiel Merritt, who were bent on capturing the pueblo of Sonoma. They knew that there would likely be no military resistance, because Vallejo had disbanded his soldiers a year earlier, after the Mexican government stopped paying them.

The insurgents went to General Vallejo's adobe compound and demanded that he surrender. Vallejo signed articles of capitulation and he was immediately sent as a prisoner to Sutter's Fort. That same day, after extensively looting the pueblo, the insurgents fashioned a home made flag featuring a grizzly bear, a red star and the words "California Republic" on its face (California's state flag is based on this design), and raised it on the flagpole in the plaza. That was the end of the bloodless "Bear Flag Revolt. The California Republic didn't last very long, however. You may remember learning in Monterey on Day Two that Commodore Sloat claimed California for the United States on July 7, 1846 during the Mexican-American War. That was just 23 days after the "Bear Flag Revolt." Old Glory was hoisted up the Sonoma Plaza flagpole three days later, on July 10. And on August 3, Commodore Sloat had Vallejo released from Sutter's fort after he had nearly starved to death. Vallejo soon lost most of his considerable wealth, but became involved in California's establishment as a member of the State Constitutional Convention, also as a State Senator.

If a military garrison stationed in this then-remote place seems like overkill, there are two reasons: First, Mexico wanted to colonize it's Alta California territory, so sent General Vallejo and his soldiers to protect its settlers. Second, Russian farmers and sea otter hunters had established a stronghold at Fort Ross, on the coast 60 miles to the northwest, and Mexico wanted them to know that they should not advance any farther south.

Interestingly, aside from the Franciscan missions which had just a few priests at each location, Mexicans were concentrated in only four California locations prior to 1846: San Diego, Los Angeles, Yerba Buena (soon to be renamed San Francisco), and Sonoma.

A Brief Walking Tour

OK, let's take a look at these historically significant buildings behind us.

....Wait just a minute! Did someone say cheese? (Is there a photographer nearby?)

Hold the history and let's visit the **Sonoma Cheese Factory** at 2 East Spain St. (#1 on the map). If you're a cheese lover—especially white cheeses—you should find this delightful and the cheeses delicious. We counted 16 different traditional and flavored "Sonoma Jack" cheeses available for tasting, and a couple of cheddars as well.

Once outside again, walk west to the next building, the **Swiss Hotel** (#2 on the map), built in 1840 as the Salvador Vallejo Adobe. (All the buildings that we'll be seeing are constructed of adobe—sun-dried bricks made of mud and straw.) This hotel building functioned as the Sonoma garrison's command post. Yes, Salvador was the brother of General Vallejo. As a captain in the Mexican army, Salvador led field operations against dissident Indian tribes, and he, also, was sent to Sutter's Fort as a prisoner on June 14, 1846.

Now, walk back to the Sonoma Cheese Factory. Here's a little-known fact: This was the site of a four-story tower, with gun ports, built by General Vallejo as an observation post. (As noted above, General Vallejo had disbanded his garrison a year earlier, so the observation tower was obviously unmanned on the day of the "Bear Flag Revolt." We're obligated to George Webber, historic re-enactor and tour guide, for this tidbit; *www.georgewebber.com*.)

Next, move to the large open space between the **Indian Servants' Quarters** (#3) and the **Toscano Hotel** (#6; known in the 1850s as Nathanson's General Store). On this site stood General Vallejo's earlier home, a two-story, 110-foot-long adobe to which the Indian Servants' Quarters was attached. Known as **Casa Grande** (#4), Vallejo and his family lived here from 1835 until they moved to Lachryma Montis in 1852. It was here that eleven of their 16 children were born, and here that the "Bear Flag Revolt" articles of capitulation were drawn up and signed. Unfortunately, the Casa Grande was destroyed by fire in April of 1867.

The **Hotel Annex** (#5) sits within this site today. The second floor of the Hotel Annex originally was a saloon that was located immediately south of the Indian Servants' Quarters. It was moved to this location, lifted, and the first floor was built underneath.

The next building to the east is **The Barracks** (#7), which offers a 22-minute historical video presentation and a bookstore to enjoy. Indians built it in stages between 1836 and 1840 under General Vallejo's direction. As the name suggests, this building housed the Mexican troops stationed with the Sonoma garrison. Following the "Bear Flag Revolt," it was used until 1852 by various U.S. military units. Step inside to see the soldiers' living quarters and a full-size replica of the Bear Flag (the original flag was destroyed in the San Francisco Earthquake/Fire of 1906). The Barracks is open daily 10am-5pm, except Thanksgiving, Christmas and New Year's Day; 707-939-9420.

The **Mission San Francisco Solano de Sonoma** (#8) is next, just across First Street East. Founded in 1823, this was last of the 21 California missions; its Padres' Quarters, joined to the east side of the chapel, is the oldest building in Sonoma. This adobe replaced the original wood chapel in 1840 by General Vallejo. There are exhibits, artifacts and paintings inside and a courtyard behind.

Across Spain St. from the Padres' Quarters is **The Blue Wing Inn** (#9). Two rooms on the first floor were built in 1840 to house Mexican soldiers who guarded the mission. In 1849, the first floor was enlarged and the second floor added, to convert the building into a saloon and hotel. Famous (and infamous) guests included bandits Three-Fingered Jack and Joaquin Murieta, future Civil War generals Grant, Longstreet and Sherman, and actress Lotta Crabtree.

Now walk west, back to the plaza, to see the **Bear Flag Monument** (#10) commemorating that event, of course. It's under the trees, inside the corner of Spain Street and First Street East.

One more building that we think you might enjoy seeing is the **City Hall** (#11), which sits commandingly in the center of the plaza. Built between 1906 and 1908, its four sides are identical—agreed to by the architect, so as to not slight any of the plaza's merchants. For more information about the area, go to the **Sonoma Valley Visitors Bureau** (#12; 707-996-1090) in the building just east of City Hall, 453 First Street East, Sonoma 95476. And if the plaza's history and architecture especially interests you, ask for the "Sonoma Walking Tour," published by the Sonoma League for Historic Preservation, that details some 55 buildings in the plaza and vicinity.

*****

ALTERNATIVE ATTRACTION IN SONOMA VALLEY

Tomorrow, on Day Seven, we'll tour the Napa Valley and some of its wineries. Alternatively, you might wish to tour the wineries (listed toward the end of Day Seven) that we've selected in the Sonoma Valley. If so, you may want to take a break from wine tasting, halfway through, and visit Jack London State Historic Park. Or this attraction may interest you more than the General Vallejo Home and Sonoma Plaza.

Jack London State Historic Park

If you're a reader of Jack London's books—among them, *The Sea Wolf*, *The Call of the Wild*, *White Fang* and *Valley of the Moon*—you may enjoy learning more about the adventurer who prospected for gold in Alaska, sailed the South Seas, served as a correspondent in the Russo-Japanese War, and was the world's most successful writer of his time. Between 1900 and 1916, his writings were popular around the world, including more than 50 books, numerous short stories, and articles on a wide range of topics.

Visit his 1,400-acre "Beauty Ranch," where you can see London's ranch buildings, the cottage where he and his wife, Charmaine, lived, his museum, and what remains of his four-story, 26-room, 15,000-square-foot dream home (that burned just before he was to move in), then take a short hike on the Lake Trail.

Open daily 10am-5pm, except Thanksgiving, Christmas and New Year's Day; 2400 London Ranch Road, Glen Ellen 95442; 707-938-5216; *www.jacklondonpark.com*.

*****

It's Dinnertime!
- **Cafe La Haye**, American/bistro cuisine, 140 E. Napa St., Sonoma, 707-935-5994, *www.cafelahaye.com*, $$.

- **Della Santina's Trattoria**, Northern Italian cuisine, 133 E. Napa St., Sonoma, 707-935-0576, *www.dellasantinas.com*, $$.
- **Deuce**, American cuisine, 691 Broadway, Sonoma, 707-933-3823, *www.dine-at-deuce.com*, $$-$$$.
- **The General's Daughter**, California cuisine, 400 West Spain St., Sonoma, 707-938-4004, *www.thegeneralsdaughter.com*, $$-$$$.
- **The Girl & the Fig** (a favorite of ours), French bistro cuisine, 110 West Spain St., Sonoma, 707-938-3634, *www.thegirlandthefig.com*, $$-$$$.
- **Glen Ellyn Inn**, California fusion cuisine, 13670 Arnold De, Glen Ellyn, 707-996-6409, *www.glenelleninn.com*, $$-$$$.
- **LaSalette**, Portuguese cuisine, 452 First St. E., Suite H, Sonoma, 707-938-1297, *www.lasalette-restaurant.com*, $$-$$$.
- **Maya Restaurant**, Latin/American cuisine, 101 E. Napa St., Sonoma, 707-935-3500, *www.mayarestaurant.com*, $$.
- **Swiss Hotel and Restaurant**, Italian cuisine, 18 West Spain St., Sonoma, 707-938-2884, *www.swisshotelsonoma.com*, $$.
- **Taste of the Himalayas**, Himalayan cuisine, 464 First St. E., Sonoma 95476, 707-996-1161, *www.himalayanexp.com*, $$.

Ginnodo-recommended B&Bs/Inns

- **Beltane Ranch**, 11775 Sonoma Hwy., 707-996-6501, *www.beltaneranch.com*, $$-$$$.
- **Brick House Bungalows Bed & Breakfast**, 313 First St. E., Sonoma 95476, 707-996-8091, fax 707-996-7301, *www.brickhousebungalows.com*, $$$.
- **The Cottage Inn and Spa-Mission B&B**, 310 First St. E., Sonoma 95476, 800-944-1490, 707-996-0719, no fax, *www.cottageinnandspa.com*, $$-$$$$.
- **Gaige House Inn**, 13540 Arnold Dr., Glen Ellen 95442, 800-935-0237, 707-935-0237, 707-935-6411, *www.gaige.com*, $$$-$$$$.
- **Hidden Oak Inn**, 214 E. Napa St., Sonoma 95476, 877-996-9863, 707-996-9863, no fax, *www.hiddenoakinn.com*, $$$.
- **Inn at Sonoma**, 630 Broadway, Sonoma 95476, 888-568-9818, 707-939-1340, fax 707-939-8834, *www.innatsonoma.com*, $$-$$$.
- **Magliulo's Rose Garden Inn**, 681 Broadway, Sonoma 95476, 707-996-1031, no fax, *www.bedandbreakfast.com/california/magliulos-rose-garden-inn*, $-$$.

- **Sonoma Chalet**, 18935 5th St. W., Sonoma 95476, 800-938-3129, 707-938-3129, fax 707-996-0190, *www.sonomachalet. com*, $$-$$$.
- **The Sonoma Hotel** (historic), 110 West Spain St., Sonoma 95476, 800-468-6016, 707-996-2996, fax 707-996-7014, *www. sonomahotel.com*, $$-$$$.
- **Thistle Dew**, 171 W. Spain St., Sonoma 95476, 800-382-7895, 707-938-2909, fax 707-938-2129, *www.thistledew.com*, $$-$$$.
- **Trojan Horse Inn**, 19455 Sonoma Hwy., Sonoma 95476, 800-899-1925, 707-996-2430, fax 707-996-9185, *www.trojanhorse inn.com*, $$$.
- **Victorian Garden Inn**, 316 E. Napa St., Sonoma 95476, 800-543-5339, 707-996-5339, fax 707-996-1689, *www.victorian gardeninn.com*, $$-$$$.

AAA- or Mobil-recommended Motels/Hotels
- **Best Western Sonoma Valley**, 550 Second St. W, Sonoma, 800-334-5784, 707-938-9200, fax 707-938-0935, *www.sonoma valleyinn.com*, $$$-$$$$.
- **El Pueblo Inn**, 896 W. Napa St., Sonoma 95476, 800-900-8844, 707-996-3651, fax 707-935-5988, *www.elpuebloinn.com*, $-$$$.
- **Ledson Hotel**, 480 First St. E., Sonoma 95476, 707-996-9779, fax 707-996-9776, *www.ledsonhotel.com*, $$$$.
- **MacArthur Place**, 29 E. MacArthur St., Sonoma 95476, 800-722-1866, 707-938-2929, *www.macarthurplace.com*, $$$-$$$$.
- **Sonoma Creek Inn**, 239 Boyes Blvd. South, Sonoma 95476, 888-712-1289, 707-939-9463, fax 707-938-3042, *www.sonoma creekinn.com*, $-$$.

Campgrounds
- **Sugarloaf Ridge State Park**, in Kenwood off Hwy 12 at the end of Adobe Canyon Road, 800-444-7275 (reservations), 707-833-5712 (details), *www.parks.ca.gov*.
- **Bothe-Napa Valley State Park**, 4 mi. south of Calistoga and 5 mi. N. of St. Helena on Hwy 29, 800-444-7275 (reservations), 707-942-4575 (details), *www.parks.ca.gov*.

Day Seven – The Wine Country

Been there, done that?

If you've previously toured the Napa Valley and want a different Wine Country experience, see the alternative excursions of the Sonoma Valley and of the Alexander/Dry Creek/Russian River Valleys later in this chapter.

If you like wine, you'll love this day! Almost all wineries are open to visitors at 10am, so you can get a little extra sleep or linger at the breakfast table this morning.

And you can enhance today's pleasure even more by visiting a favorite winery along the way. Check with your innkeeper or front desk person for the address and directions to that winery, or look for it on one of the Web sites listed later in this chapter (under "Alternate Wine Country Excursions").

If you're sticking with the Napa Valley tour, here's what we have in store for you. Visiting four or five of the valley's 200 wineries makes for a full day; so we've selected the ones that we would want to visit if this were our first trip to the Wine Country.

We'll start with a winery visit that includes a guided tour. We're suggesting that you choose among Domaine Chandon, Cakebread Cellars and Robert Mondavi Winery, so you'll have that special experience. *During the summer and fall, advance reservations are usually needed for the Cakebread and Robert Mondavi tours; we suggest that you make them as far ahead as possible.*

If you're unable to arrange a tour, these wineries are "class" operations and are good to visit anyway. Of course, you'll have the opportunity to taste wines at all the wineries we visit today. After the guided tour, we point you to the unique Oakville Grocery, and then to V. Sattui Winery for a picnic lunch under their beautiful spreading oaks.

This afternoon, we'll visit Sutter Home where you'll enjoy strolling through the gardens of their stately Victorian mansion. Next, we'll view the castle and Chinese gardens at Chateau Montelena and the architecture and art at Clos Pegase. Then, we'll enjoy a ride in an overhead tram, a wonderful inside self-guided tour, and fine wine tasting at Sterling Vineyards.

We'll wrap up the day with a stroll around the town of Calistoga, dinner at one of our favorite restaurants, and, finally, a stroll around St. Helena.

If you want more choices, contact the Napa Valley Conference and Visitors Bureau, 1310 Napa Town Center, Napa, CA 94559; 707-226-7459; *www.napavalley.org.* (Ask for the Napa Valley Guidebook.)

A caution: multiple wine tastings can lead to slowed reflexes, so please eat something between tastings and drive with care, or appoint a designated driver!

A Brief Wine Primer

If you're a wine sophisticate, you may want to skip this section and go directly to the next. What we hope to do now is briefly prepare non- or occasional wine drinkers for their tasting experiences.

Consider the grapevine. The Franciscan priests who established California's missions during the 1700's brought a pedestrian variety of grape to the area from Mexico. During the 1800's, European varieties were imported, and along with them came a root-chewing insect called phylloxera, which devastated most of the vineyards of Europe and America. Thanks to the bug-resistant California grapevines, onto which other varieties were grafted, European and American wine making was able to survive.

"Thrive" is a better word for what happened in the Napa Valley—a 29-mile-long valley with ideal soil and weather conditions. It produces some of the best wines in the world.

There will be several opportunities today for you to learn about the winemaking process, so we'll leave that educational task mostly to the wineries themselves. In a nutshell, however, it involves *planting* the vines, *growing* and *harvesting* the grapes, *pressing* the juice from the grapes, *fermenting* the juice in wooden casks or stainless-steel vats, and *bottling* the processed wine. Fermentation, which is the conversion of fruit sugar into alcohol, is caused by bringing the juice into contact with yeasts on the skins of ripe grapes.

White wine is made mostly from light-colored grape varieties such as Chardonnay, Chenin Blanc, Gewurztraminer, Riesling and Sauvignon Blanc. When red grapes are used for white wine, the skins are removed before they can color the juice.

Red wine is made from dark-colored grape varieties such as Cabernet Sauvignon, Gamay, Grenache, Merlot, Pinot Noir, Syrah (Shiraz), and Zinfandel. In the making of red wine, the grape skins and seeds are kept in contact with the juice throughout fermentation, giving the wine its greater depth of color and taste. The sharp taste that's experienced, to varying degrees, in red wine comes from chemicals called "tannins" which are found in grape skins, seeds and stalks.

Tannins are important in the aging of red wines, that is, in bringing them to peak maturity.

White wines and light-bodied reds generally have little tannin and require less aging before consumption.

Wines made from a single variety of grape are referred to as "varietals"; those made from two or more varieties are called "blends."

White wines are usually classified as dry (without sweetness), medium, or sweet. Almost all red wines are dry.

Both whites and reds are characterized as light-bodied, medium-bodied, or full-bodied. This has to do with the wine's consistency, or thinness.

What we've done below is arranged the white varietals that you're most likely to encounter in the tasting rooms from dry to sweet:

> Sauvignon Blanc - dry, light-bodied
> Chardonnay - dry, medium-bodied and full-bodied
> Chenin Blanc - medium, light-bodied
> Riesling - medium, light-bodied
> Gewurztraminer - semi-sweet, medium-bodied

And we've arranged the red varietals from light- to full-bodied:

> Gamay - light (used in making Beaujolais)
> Grenache - light
> Zinfandel - medium
> Merlot - medium
> Cabernet sauvignon - medium
> Pinot Noir (Burgundy) - full
> Syrah (Shiraz) - full and often robust

Bordeaux wines are not listed because they are a blend, usually of Cabernet Sauvignon and Merlot.

If you're wondering where port wine, sherry, vermouth and dessert wine fit into this classification, the answer is: they don't. All are fortified blends; that is, a grape-based sweetening agent is added to the juices of two or more grape varieties just before or after the end of fermentation. Vermouth also has herbs and spices added. Dessert wines are made from grapes that are picked late to maximize sweetness and then are heated and cooled after fermentation.

Champagne, or sparkling wine, is made from Chardonnay and Pinot Noir grapes during a second fermentation in bottles after yeasts and sugars are added. Tiny bubbles result during the second fermentation, or when carbon dioxide is injected.

The term "reserve wine" is reserved (pun intended) for that winery's best output.

Now let's get to the best part: wine-tasting.

So that you can better taste the flavors of the more subtle wines, the "general rule" is to sample white before red, dry before sweet, and light before full bodied.

Wine tasting is basically a simple four-step process:

1. *Examine* the color and clarity of the wine in the glass.

2. Gently *swirl* the wine in the glass and take a deep *sniff* of its aroma. Taste, as you know, is heavily influenced by smell.

3. Take in a small amount and *roll it* around your mouth. The idea is to expose the wine to the back, top, tip and sides of the tongue where different taste sensations occur.

4. *Swallow,* and *assess* the aftertaste; that is, the continuation of the aroma and flavor in your mouth after swallowing.

If you keep these things in mind as you visit the wineries and sample their products, you'll move one step closer to being a connoisseur of wines.

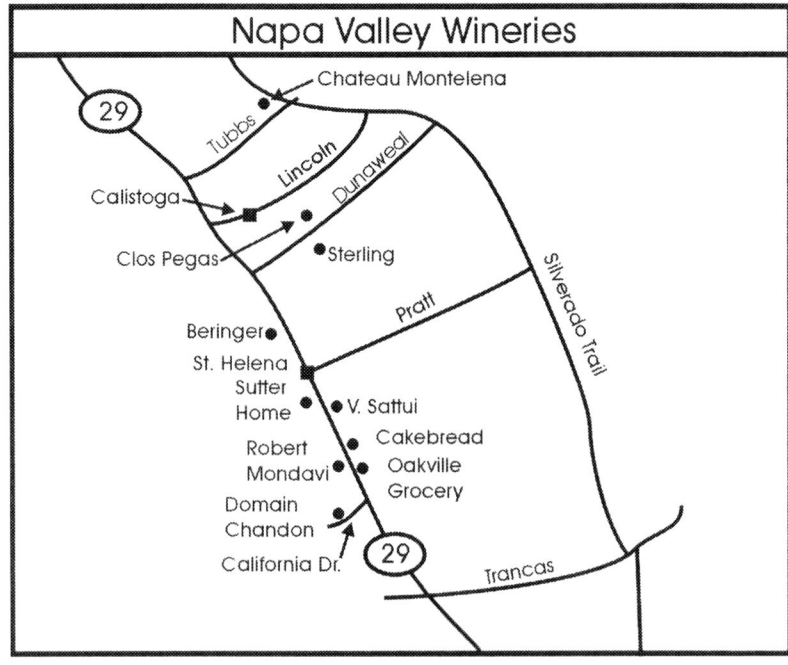

Choose Your Guided Winery Tour

We've enjoyed, and highly recommend, the guided tour at Domaine Chandon, the "In Depth Tour and Tasting" at Cakebread Cellars, and the "Vineyard and Winery Tour" at Robert Mondavi.

Domaine Chandon's inside tour is 35 minutes long and shows the entire manufacturing and bottling process. It's very educational for newbies to champagne making. The tour is complimentary, does not require a reservation, and departs from the visitor center at 11am, 1pm and 3pm Sunday through Friday, and at 11am, and 1, 3 and 5pm on Saturday. There is a fee, if you wish to taste.

Cakebread's complimentary tour of the vineyard periphery and the winemaking process is given once daily, at 10:30am, and lasts approximately 90 minutes. It includes a complimentary wine tasting in the courtyard (instead of the tasting room). The tasting room is open from 10am-4pm, and there is a tasting fee. You do the math: the tour is a better deal than going to the tasting room. But a reservation is necessary (by telephoning 707-963-5222 in advance).

The Robert Mondavi tour into the vineyards and the winemaking process takes about 75 minutes. There is a fee for the tour, which includes tasting. Tours depart on the hour from 10am-4pm, and we recommend that you arrive at least ten minutes early to sign in and pay for the tour. Because of the popularity of Robert Mondavi's tour, during the summer and fall you should make a reservation in advance at 888-766-6328, extension 2000.

Notice the start times of the three tours: Domaine Chandon at 11am; Cakebread at 10:30am; Robert Mondavi at 10 or 11am. If this were our first time to Napa Valley, we would arrive at Domaine Chandon a little before their 10am opening, examine the lighted display of the champagne-making process in the hallway, and drive three and a half miles north to tour either Cakebread at 10:30am or Robert Mondavi at 11am.

Domaine Chandon

Owned by Moet Hennessy Louis Vuitton of France, Domaine Chandon is Napa Valley's best-known producer of champagne. If you can't join a tour, be sure to see the lighted display of the champagne-making process in the hallway. The winery's French cuisine restaurant is on everyone's list of the best places to eat in the Napa Valley; it's open for lunch and dinner. Interestingly, Domaine Chandon also produces regular (non-bubbly) varietals that are only available in the restaurant, shop, or by mail and Internet.

Open daily 10am-6pm (Nov-Apr, Wed-Sun, 10am-6pm); inside complimentary tour as described four paragraphs above; tasting fee; 1 California Drive, Yountville 94559; 707-944-2280; *www.chandon.com.*

Cakebread Cellars

This winery is a bit difficult to find because it's small, unpretentious and the identifying sign is hard to see. Just after you pass Robert Mondavi (on the left) heading north on Highway 29, you'll see Opus One Winery and Turnbull Wine Cellars on your right. Cakebread Cellars is the first winery past Turnbull. Turn in at the black mailbox (if you reach Sequoia Grove Vineyards, you've gone too far).

We love the informal-but-classy aura and sense of quality about this winery. The tour is intimate and excellently done. (And the wine is good, too!) We particularly enjoyed learning how the Cakebread family acquired the land from a cattle rancher in 1973 and started their winery.

Open daily 10am-4pm; complimentary 90-minute tour of vineyard and production facility at 10:30am (includes tasting; call ahead); tasting fee in tasting room; 8300 St. Helena Hwy (Hwy. 29), Rutherford 94573; 707-963-5222 or 800-588-0298; *www.cakebread.com.*

Robert Mondavi Winery

The first thing you'll notice is Robert Mondavi's lovely, sweeping architecture. From its front entrance to the inside layout, the winery resembles a modernesque California mission. This is one of the Napa Valley's "anchor" wineries; that is, it's widely known and draws many visitors to the area. One reason for its popularity is that from the time he founded the winery in 1966, Robert Mondavi's goal was to educate the public about wine. This led, among other things, to the offering of several different kinds of tours, picnics in the vineyard, a summer music series and The Great Chefs at Robert Mondavi Winery series. The winery was purchased in December 2004 by Constellation Brands, a major producer and marketer of alcoholic beverages.

The 75-minute guide-led tour starts in the demonstration vineyards with a description of how grapes are grown and harvested, then proceeds to the grape presses, aging cellars, bottling area and private tasting room. After the tour and tasting, see the art gallery down the walkway from the tour reception desk.

Open daily 10am-5pm; vineyard tours on the hour, 10am-4pm; the tour fee includes an excellent sit-down tasting; 7801 St. Helena Hwy. (Hwy. 29), Oakville 94562; 888-766-6328; *www.robertmondavi.com.*

Oakville Grocery

This Napa Valley institution is almost directly across the street from the entrance to the Robert Mondavi Winery. We suggest a brief walk-through of this combination grocery store-delicatessen before you head north to our next winery.

Built in 1881 to serve the mercantile needs of Oakville, the grocery has fed and pleased locals and visitors alike for more than 125 years. The Oakville Grocery has also opened stores in Healdsburg and Palo Alto, California.

If you purchase a sandwich here, please don't plan to eat it at V. Sattui, which has its own excellent delicatessen, and, understandably, does not appreciate the consumption of others' food on their grounds.

Open daily 9am-5pm; 7856 St. Helena Hwy. (Hwy. 29), Oakville 94562; 707-944-8802; *www.oakvillegrocery.com.*

V. Sattui

We can't imagine a more pleasant commercial picnic environment than this one, despite the presence of so many people.

Inside, you'll find a wonderful delicatessen and a tasting room (there's no tasting fee). V. Sattui's wines are sold only at the winery, by mail order, or from their website. There are condiments and cheeses to sample, and you have three choices for lunch: 1) "go European" by purchasing bread, cheese, fruit and wine; 2) buy chicken, ribs, and prepared vegetables delicatessen-style; or 3) buy delicious ready-made sandwiches. Ask for a package of utensils and napkins at the cash registers. Then take your picnic outside to the lawns and tables under two-and-a-half acres of spreading oaks; relax, and enjoy.

Architecturally, this winery is a very pretty place. The delicatessen and tasting room are in the original winery building. The second stone building, in the Italian Romanesque style, was built in 1985. Be sure to visit the cellars and historical museum under this building. You'll learn how Vitorrio Sattui established the winery (in San Francisco) in 1885 and his great-grandson, Daryl Sattui, reopened it in the Napa Valley in 1976.

Open daily 9am-6pm (closes 5pm Nov-Feb); 111 White Lane, St. Helena 94574; 707-963-7774 or 800-799-2337; *www.vsattui.com.*

Time Check

It's early afternoon and there are four wineries and two charming towns to visit. It's unlikely that you can experience all of them *fully* before the Calistoga area wineries close.

As we see it, you have three choices: 1) you can hurry through our tour as written in order to get it all in, 2) you can drop a winery or two, or 3) you can save time at a couple of wineries by omitting the tastings. We would opt for the third choice. You may want to read ahead in order to decide on your priorities.

Remember, our primary objective is to get you on the aerial tram at Sterling Vineyards by 4:30pm. Sterling is a winery experience that should not be missed.

After Sterling, you can stroll around Calistoga, enjoy a beautiful drive down the Silverado Trail, savor a good meal at one of our recommended restaurants, and admire St. Helena after dinner.

Sutter Home/Trinchero Family Estates Winery

Yes, if you're wondering, this winery, which dates from 1874, was named for John Sutter of gold-discovery fame. It's been owned and run by the Trinchero family since 1947.

At this stop you'll admire the Victorian mansion (from outside only) and enjoy a walk through the winery's gardens, which contain 40 varieties of day lilies, 100 varieties of roses, palm trees from the Canary Islands, and a 130 year-old camellia at the mansion's entrance.

Sutter Home's claim to fame is it's innovative White Zinfandel that became the best-selling wine in the United States in the 1980's. Another innovation is the winery's unusual line of alcohol-free wines bottled under the Fre label. We particularly enjoyed the Montevina Zinfandel and a delicious proprietary triple-cream sherry that's available only at the winery. Take a look around the tasting room; you'll find some interesting food and gift items for sale.

Open daily 9am-5pm; tasting of three wines is complimentary; 277 St. Helena Hwy. (Hwy 29), St. Helena 94574; 707-963-3104 or 800-967-4663; *www.sutterhome.com* and *www.trincherofamilyestates.com.*

Beringer and the Culinary Institute

We'll drive by both of these "institutions," on your left, shortly after leaving St. Helena. We thought that you'd like to know a little something about them.

Seen from the row of elms on Highway 29, Beringer Vineyards, with its 17-room mansion, looks like an estate on the Rhine River. For good reason: it's a copy of the Beringer family home in Germany, built after the winery was established in 1876. The setting, lawns and gardens make this one of the most picturesque wineries in the Napa Valley. One interesting fact: wines are aged and stored behind the mansion in tunnels that were hand-chiseled 250 feet into the rock by Chinese who had worked on the transcontinental railroad. Beringer, now owned by the Nestle Corporation, claims the distinction of being "the oldest Napa Valley winery in continuous operation."

Less than a quarter-mile farther, you'll come upon the western campus of the Culinary Institute of America (headquartered in Hyde Park, New York). Previously a winery owned by Christian Brothers, and then Heublein, the property is now used to train future chefs in 15,000 square feet of teaching kitchens. It also houses The Wine Spectator Greystone Restaurant and a store that sells everything imaginable for the kitchen. The students do not manage or staff the restaurant. The CIA's seven garden terraces supply the teaching kitchens and restaurant with organic culinary herbs.

If you look to the right about seven miles after passing the Culinary Institute, you'll see the white Mediterranean-style buildings of Sterling Vineyards perched on a 300-foot knoll. From that high vantage point, you'll soon be enjoying one of the best views in the Napa Valley.

But, for now, if there's time, we'll drive on to Chateau Montelena, about three and a half miles farther up Highway 29, near the end of Tubbs Lane.

Chateau Montelena

The name suggests a castle near a mountain. And that's what it is. The French-style stone chateau, built in the early 1880's by the winery's founder, Albert L. Tubbs, is situated at the base of Mount St. Helena (4,343 ft). But the property didn't attain its current level of beauty until the Frank family purchased the winery in 1958. They excavated Jade Lake and installed Chinese gardens with red-lacquered pavilions and colorful bridges connecting several islands. Do take a walk down to see them.

The winery earned its reputation from a formal Parisian blind tasting in 1976. In it, nine French wine experts judged four French white Burgundies against six California Pinot Chardonnays, and Chateau Montelena's 1973 Chardonnay won top honors. Interestingly, the Stags Leap Wine Cellars entry (also in the Napa Valley, on the Silverado Trail) was the top-scoring red wine at the same tasting. Suddenly, California wines ranked right up there with the best wines from France.

Open daily 9:30am-4pm; tasting fee; 1-1/2 hour guided tours for a fee at 2pm available by advance reservation; 1429 Tubbs Lane, Calistoga 94515; 707-942-5105; *www.chateaumontelena.com.*

Now, backtrack on Tubbs Lane and Highway 29 to Dunaweal Lane, where you'll find Clos Pegase across from Sterling Vineyards. Time permitting, do stop at Clos Pegas to enjoy its architectural and artistic delights.

Clos Pegase

From a design and artistic standpoint, Clos Pegase is the most avant-garde of the Napa Valley wineries. Architect Michael Graves designed this "Post-modern temple to wine and art." Outside, from the parking lot to the inner courtyard, you'll see some interesting sculptures and architecture. Inside, the winery's art collection is scattered throughout the tasting room. You can also ask to go into the offices to see the artwork there.

Open daily 10:30am-5pm; tasting fee; 1060 Dunaweal Lane, Calistoga 94515; 707-942-4981 x213; *www.clospegase.com* .

Sterling (See the photograph at the front of this book.)

You'll need to arrive at Sterling and be in line (if any) by 4:30pm in order to enter the winery. You can tour and taste at your leisure; you will not be rushed.

Sterling's aerial tram is a unique and beautiful way to enter a winery. Once in the winery, you'll enjoy the panoramic view of the valley from the terrace, as well as Sterling's excellent self-guided tour of winemaking operations viewed from elevated platforms. Interesting descriptions at every stage of the winemaking process make this a very educational tour.

The tasting experience is also unique. Weather permitting, you'll be seated outside on the deck, under the trees, served by a very pleasant and professional staff. Sterling's Napa Valley Merlot is the best Merlot we've ever tasted.

Open daily 10:30am-4:30pm; the entrance fee includes tram, self-guided winery tour, and tasting; 1111 Dunaweal Lane, Calistoga 94515; 707-942-3344; *www.sterlingvineyards.com.*

Calistoga

To get to Calistoga, return to Highway 29, turn right, and drive a little over a mile to Lincoln, where you'll turn right. This is a town with a laid-back western look and feel. Our guess is that you'll be ready for dinner about this time, so won't want to stop; but you might find a brief walkaround to be a nice change of pace.

Do you remember Sam Brannan who spread the word about the Coloma gold discovery and became California's first millionaire selling supplies to miners? Well, it was he who laid out the town of Calistoga in 1859 and started the resort spa industry that thrives in the area today. (Alas, Sam didn't continue to thrive; he died in poverty near San Diego in 1888.)

If You're Spending the Night in the Santa Rosa Area: In Calistoga on Hwy. 29, turn left on Petrified Forest Rd., just north of Lincoln, and follow the signs into Santa Rosa. Petrified Forest Rd. runs into Porter Creek Rd., which runs into Mark West Springs Rd., which intersects with I-101 in North Santa Rosa.

Return to St. Helena via the Silverado Trail

Simply continue east on Lincoln a half mile or so to the Silverado Trail and turn right. About nine miles south, turn right onto Pratt to cross back over to Highway 29 and St. Helena.

You'll only see the top third of the Silverado Trail, but it's a beautiful, peaceful and quick drive. There are quite a few Napa Valley wineries on the Silverado Trail, but most of them are south of Pratt.

St. Helena

St. Helena is a town where residents shop, buy and eat locally, mixing with the tourists, who enjoy it as well. Its few blocks of downtown are homey but classy, and busy but relaxed. The town runs the gamut from down-home shops to pricey boutiques. In other words, it has the feel of Main Street America of 30 or 40 years ago, with overtones of elegance. Soak up the ambiance!

Our choice would be to first have dinner, then stroll St. Helena's downtown—unless the shops are still open and you need to scratch the shopping itch before dinner. (Most shops close at 5 and 6 p.m.)

*****

Please see our warning in the "What You Should Know" section, at the front of the book, about the need to make lodging and restaurant reservations in advance of your arrival in the Wine Country.

It's Dinnertime!

In St. Helena:

- **Cindy's Backstreet Kitchen**, California cuisine, 1327 Railroad Ave., 707-963-1200, *www.cindysbackstreetkitchen.com*, $$.
- **Press**, American cuisine, 587 Hwy 29, 707-967-0550 or fax 707-967-0440, *www.presssthelena.com*, $$$.
- **Taylor's Refresher**, drive-in style, 933 Main St., 707-963-3486, no Web site-consult Google, $-$$.
- **Terra**, French/Italian cuisine, 1345 Railroad Ave., 707-963-8931, *www.terrarestaurant.com*, $$$.
- **Tra Vigne** (a favorite of ours), Italian cuisine, 1050 Charter Oak, 707-963-4444, *www.travignerestaurant.com*, $$-$$$

In Yountville (notable restaurants seven miles south of St. Helena):

- **Bouchon**, French cuisine, 6534 Washington St., 707-944-8037, *www.opentable.com*, $$$$.
- **Brix**, California cuisine, 7377 St. Helena Hwy., 707-944-2749 or fax 707-944-8320,*www.brix.com*, $$$-$$$$.
- **Domaine Chandon**, French cuisine, One California Blvd., 707-944-2892, *www.chandon.com*, $$$-$$$$.
- **The French Laundry**, American/French menu, 6640 Washington Ave., 707-944-2380, *www.frenchlaundry.com*, $$$$.
- **Mustards Grill**, California cuisine, 7399 St. Helena Hwy., 707-944-2424 or fax 707-944-0828, *www.mustardsgrill.com*, $$-$$$.

Ginnodo-recommended B&Bs/Inns

Some require a two-night minimum, especially on weekends.

- **Adagio Inn**, 1417 Kearney St., St. Helena 94574, 800-8ADAGIO, 707-963-2238, fax 707-963-5598, *www.adagioinn.com*, $$$-$$$$.
- **Ambrose Bierce House**, 1515 Main St., St. Helena 94574, 707-963-3003, fax 707-963-9367, *www.ambrosebiercehouse.com*, $$$.
- **Forest Manor**, 415 Cold Springs Rd., St. Helena 94508, 800-788-0364, 707-965-3538, *www.forestmanor.com*, $$$-$$$$.
- **Harvest Inn**, One Main St., St. Helena 94574, 800-950-8466, 707-963-9463, fax 707-963-4402, *www.harvestinn.com*, $$$$.
- **Ink House**, 1575 St. Helena Hwy., St. Helena 94574, 707-963-3890, *www.inkhouse.com*, $$-$$$.

- **Inn at Southbridge**, 1020 Main St., St. Helena 94574, 800-520-6800, 707-967-9400, fax 707-967-9486, *www.innatsouth bridge.com*, $$$$.
- **Shady Oaks Country Inn**, 399 Zinfandel Ln., St. Helena 94574, 707-963-1190, fax 707-963-9367, *www.shadyoaksinn. com*, $$$.
- **Vineyard Country Inn**, 201 Main St., St. Helena 94574, 707-963-1000, fax 707-963-1794, *www.vineyardcountryinn.com*, $$-$$$.
- **Wine Country Inn**, 1152 Lodi Ln., St. Helena 94574, 888-465-4608, 707-963-7077, fax 707-963-9018, *www.winecountryinn. com*, $$$-$$$$.

AAA- or Mobil-recommended Accommodations
- **El Bonita Motel**, 195 Main St., St. Helena 94574, 800-541-3284, 707-963-3216, fax 707-963-8838, *www.elbonita.com*, $$-$$$.
- **Hotel St. Helena**, 1309 Main St., St. Helena 94574, 888-478-4355, 707-963-4388, fax 707-963-5402, *www.hotelsthelena. com*, $$-$$$.

Campgrounds
- **Bothe-Napa Valley State Park**, 4 mi. south of Calistoga and 5 mi. N of St. Helena on Hwy 29, 800-444-7275 (reservations), 707-942-4575 (details), *www.parks.ca.gov*.
- **Sugarloaf Ridge State Park**, in Kenwood off Hwy 12 at the end of Adobe Canyon Road, 800-444-7275 (reservations), 707-833-5712 (details), *www.parks.ca.gov*.

*****

Alternative Wine Country Excursions
We've tried to approximate the Napa Valley "wine experience" in the two following excursions. What we mean by that is, we've selected wineries in each area that have "something extra," such as a vineyard tour, picnic area, gardens, distinctive architecture, interesting history, etc. Instead of simply hopping from one wine tasting to another, you'll have the opportunity and time to enjoy the eclectic aura of California's wine country.

We had the assistance of knowledgeable locals in selecting these wineries, and we've confirmed their excellence during personal visits.

If you are a novice or occasional wine drinker you may find the "Brief Wine Primer" earlier in this chapter to be of value before you begin touring and tasting.

Generally, there is a wine tasting fee in Sonoma Valley wineries, which is often waived with a purchase. In contrast, wine tasting is often complimentary in the Alexander/Dry Creek/Russian River Valley area.

Please remember that wine tastings can lead to slowed reflexes; so eat something between tastings, be especially cautious as you drive, or appoint a designated driver.

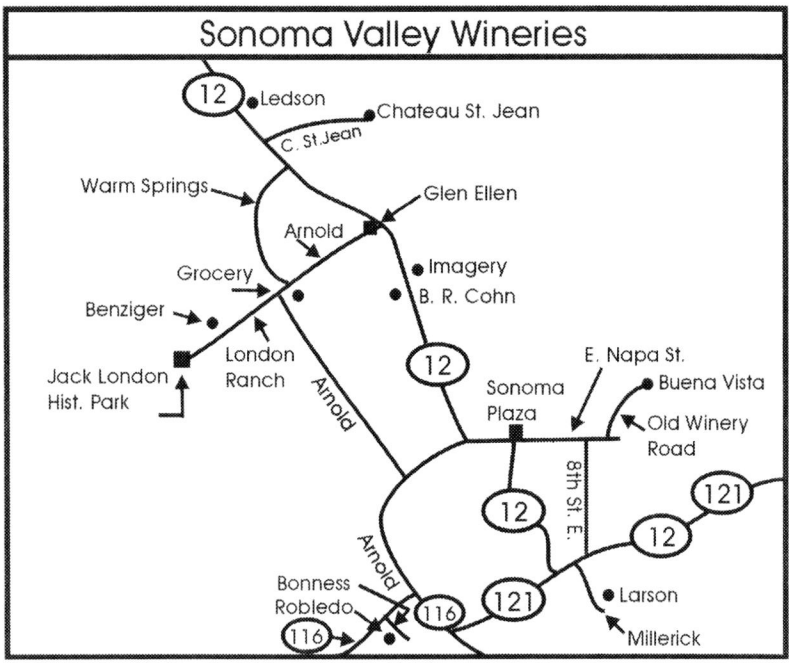

SONOMA VALLEY EXCURSION

So that you have some choice, we provide information here on eight selected wineries in the Sonoma Valley. While it's possible to visit all eight in one day, we recommend that you limit yourself to only five; otherwise, you may find yourself rushing and not enjoying. So, our suggestion is: read through all the descriptions and settle on the ones that most appeal to you. They are arranged in sequence from south to north, so that no matter which ones you choose, your progression from one winery to the next should be fairly smooth. In our opinion, the

Benziger vineyard tram tour and Chateau St. Jean's architecture and gardens should not be missed.

We also recommend that you buy sandwiches at the Glen Ellen Village Market and eat lunch at one of three picnic areas. And we suggest the Jack London State Historic Park as a nice change of pace. Accommodations and restaurants in the Sonoma Valley are listed in the prior chapter. For more choices, contact the Sonoma Valley Visitors Bureau, 453 First Street East, Sonoma, CA 95476, 707-996-1090, *www.sonomavalley.com.* (Ask for the Sonoma Valley Visitors Guide.)

Buena Vista Historic Winery
This is where European-style wine making began in California. Read the outside display boards, opposite the tasting room, to learn about grape growing in this cooler Carneros microclimate, and how Hungarian Agoston Haraszthy was the first (in 1857) to replace the pedestrian mission grape with grapes from France and Germany. Try the Pinot Noir, Merlot and Chardonnay. Open weekdays 10am to 5pm, Saturday and Sunday 10am-5:30pm; 18000 Old Winery Rd., Sonoma 95476; 707-265-1472; *www.buenavistawinery.com.*

Robledo Family Winery
This is the first winery established in America (1997) by a Mexican migrant vineyard worker. All nine Robledo children are involved in the operation. Their story is told in the August 2005 *People* magazine. The winery is in the Carneros Region, which is influenced by Pacific Ocean and San Francisco Bay weather. Try the Pinot Noir, Syrah and Sauvignon Blanc. Open Monday through Saturday 10am to 5pm and Sunday 11am to 4pm; 21901 Bonness Rd., Sonoma 95476; 707-939-6903, *www.robledofamilywinery.com.*

Larson Family Winery/Sonoma Creek
Also family-owned (since the 1860s) and located in the Carneros Region, this winery was the site of the Sonoma Rodeo from 1920 to the early 1950's, and exhibits plenty of rodeo memorabilia to prove it. Steamboats once called here from Oakland. See Dollie Llama and Lucky Lamb, play bocci ball. Try the Gewurztraminer. Open daily 10am-5pm; 23355 Millerick Rd., Sonoma 95476; 707-938-3031; *www.larsonfamilywinery.com.*

Lunchtime in the Glen Ellen Area

Buy your deli lunch at the Glen Ellen Village Market, 13751 Arnold Drive. This market features the best delicatessen that we've ever seen, and the ready-made sandwiches are super-delicious. Picnic at: Benziger (shaded, with the most seating), B.R. Cohn (a wonderful patio), or Imagery (sunny tables in both front and back of the winery).

B.R. Cohn

Here, you'll find not only vineyards, but also a 130-year old olive grove. Not surprisingly, they sell wines, olive oils and vinegars. The winery's owner was the Dooby Brothers road manager. There are also a stage for large benefit concerts and a patio area for picnics. They specialize in Cabernet Sauvignon. Open daily 10am to 5pm; 15000 Sonoma Hwy., Glen Ellen, 95442; 707-938-4064; *www.brcohn.com.*

Imagery Estate Winery

Owned by Benziger, Imagery commissions artists to create new labels each year and displays 170 original pieces of label art displayed around the tasting room and in the gallery, thus claiming the world's largest wine label art collection. Outside, on the "Appellation Trail," be sure to read the descriptions of a dozen varietals in the showcases. Although wines are distributed only to California restaurants and wine shops, they can be purchased in the tasting room and online. Try the Malbec and White Burgundy. Open daily 10am-4:30pm; 14335 Sonoma Hwy., Glen Ellen, 95442; 707-935-4500; *www.imagerywinery.com.*

Benziger Family Winery

Exceptional are the 45-minute tractor-pulled tram tour through vineyards, a visit to the wine caves, and the included wine tasting. In summertime, be sure to reserve in advance at 888-490-2739. The winery is known for its organic wines; try the Sonoma Mountain Red, Tribute, and Chardonnay. Open daily 10am-5pm; 1883 London Ranch Rd., Glen Ellen 95442; 707-935-3000; *www.benziger.com.*

Jack London State Historic Park

This is an opportunity for some diversion and also to learn about one of the world's most successful writers. For a description of this park, see "Alternative Attraction in Sonoma Valley" near the end of the last chapter (Day Six).

Chateau St. Jean

This is a gorgeous French chateau setting, with formal gardens, an expansive green lawn, fishponds, an arched footbridge, and fountains. There's a small deli inside. We recommend that you pay the extra $5 to taste in the Vineyard reserve room, so that you can try any of the Cinqs and the Robert Young Vineyard Reserve Chardonnay. Open daily 10am-5pm; 8555 Sonoma Hwy., Kenwood, 95452; 707-833-4134; *www.chateaustjean.com.*

Ledson Winery & Vineyards

Known locally as "The Castle," this property and its French Normandy-inspired architecture are impressive. (The winery also owns the Ledson Hotel and Harmony Club in Sonoma.) Try the Zinfandel, Merlot and Sauvignon Blanc. Open daily 10am-5pm; 7335 Sonoma Hwy., Kenwood, 95409; 707-833-2330; *www.ledson.com.*

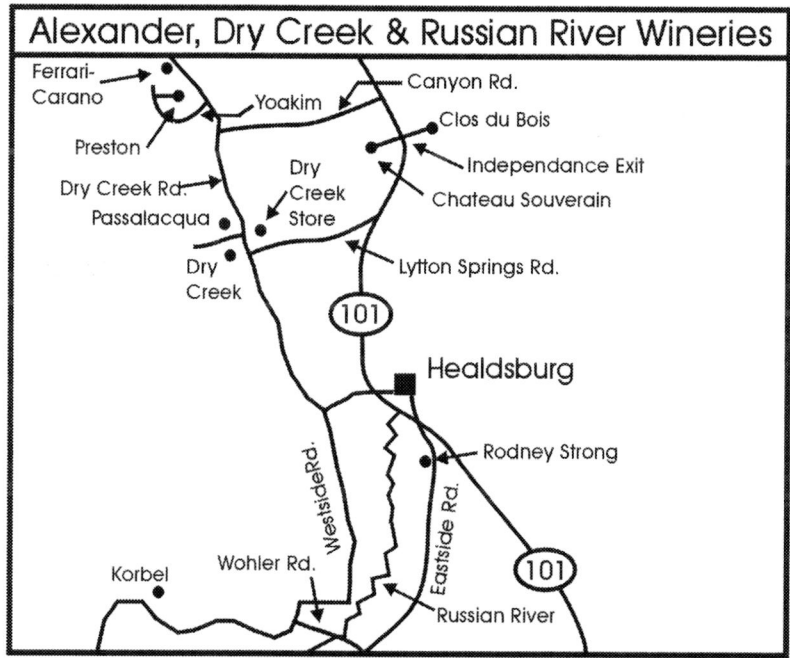

ALEXANDER, DRY CREEK, AND RUSSIAN RIVER VALLEYS EXCURSION

We recommend that you spend some time perusing this particular Web site beforehand: *www.visitwineroad.com/daytrips.htm.* We think you'll agree that it is well worth the time; and it's all free! It lists more than 100 wineries and many lodgings, with descriptions, maps, addresses, hours, links to their Web pages—and much more.

Here's a helpful tidbit from this Web site:

The wineries of the Wine Road, with their coastal and inland growing regions, distinct microclimates and soils, have the immense good fortune to be able to produce spectacular harvests of many different grape varietals. Even though the growing appellations within the Wine Road are famous for certain varietals—Russian River Valley for Pinot Noir and Chardonnay, Dry Creek Valley for Zinfandel and Sauvignon Blanc, and Alexander Valley for Cabernet and Merlot—there are dozens of other varietals grown in all these regions. Barbera, Grenache, Riesling, Gewurztraminer, Mourvedre, Cinsault, Carignane, Dolcetto, Sangiovese and Petite Sirah (to name a few), are as much at home here as Cabernet Franc, Syrah, Pinot Blanc, Semilion and Viognier.

After viewing the Wine Road Web site, you may choose an entirely different set of wineries to visit than the ones that follow, and that's just fine with us. Create your own wonderful day of touring and tasting!

Nevertheless, here are the eight wineries that we selected and visited with the help of a local expert. As with the Sonoma Valley excursion, it is possible to visit all eight, but again we feel that visiting just five wineries in a day is more realistic and avoids rushing and not enjoying. So, we suggest that you read through the following descriptions and choose the wineries that most appeal to you. They are arranged in sequence from north to south, to avoid backtracking. In our opinion, Chateau Souverain and Ferrari-Carano are not to be missed; their gardens and architecture are truly spectacular.

If you plan to spend the night in this wine region, we suggest that you peruse the accommodations listed on the Wine Road Web site (see above).

Clos du Bois Wines

This large winery has six acres of production and administrative facilities under roof. Try the Sonoma Coast Pinot Noir, Marlston and Reserve Chardonnay. Open daily 10am to 4:30pm; 19410 Geyserville Ave., Geyserville, 95441; 707-857-3100; *www.closdubois.com.*

Chateau Souverain (See the photograph at the front of this book.)

The entrance and grounds of Chateau Souverain are spectacular, as are the French chateau and fountain courtyard with its exceptional rose garden. There is a great view from the outdoor terrace, and don't miss the paintings in the corridor between the tasting room and the restaurant. Try the Reserve Cabernet, Chardonnay, and Sauvignon Blanc (a personal favorite of ours). Open daily 10am to 5pm, except Christmas and New Year's Days; 400 Souverain Rd., Geyersville, 95441; 707-433-3141; *www.chateausauverain.com.*

Ferrari-Carano Vineyards & Winery

This breathtaking winery showcases deep green lawns, eye-popping red flowers and a beautiful Italian villa. Be sure to enter through the wrought-iron gate near the tasting room, and follow the path through the winery's five acres of gardens. Try the Siena (a "super Tuscan" blend of reds), Fume Blanc and Alexander Valley Chardonnay. Open daily 10am to 5pm; 8761 Dry Creek Rd., Healdsburg, 95448; 707-433-6700; *www.ferrari-carano.com.*

Preston Vineyards

Preston is small, homey, dusty, and architecturally challenged, but it does have fresh bread from its own bakery and 1,000 olive trees from which they make their own olive oil and brined olives. Their wine is distributed only in California. They make a red and a white; try them both. Open daily 11am-4:30pm; 9282 W. Dry Creek Rd., Healdsburg, 95448; 707-433-3372; *www.prestonvineyards.com.*

Dry Creek General Store

The store is located on Dry Creek Rd. just north of Lytton Springs Rd. Stop here and purchase a delicious deli sandwich to go. Then, cross the road to Passalacqua.

Passalacqua Winery

Family owned and operated, this is a great place to eat your deli lunch. Head for the tables down the hill, under jasmine and wisteria; they are a hidden treasure...a great setting, panoramic view and protected if there's any wind. Stroll by the redwood-shaded veranda, gardens, stone fountains and koi pond. Try the Zinfandel and Cabernet Sauvignon. Open daily 11am-5pm; 3805 Lambert Bridge Rd., Healdsburg, 95448; 887-825-5547; *www.passalacquawinery.com.*

Dry Creek Vineyard

You'll find Dry Creek next door to Passalacqua. They also have a nicely shaded picnic area. This winery is known for its flagship Fume

Blanc. Try the Fume as well as the Zinfandel and Meritage. Open daily 10:30am to 4:30pm; 3770 Lambert Bridge Rd., Healdsburg, CA 95448; 707-433-1000; www.*drycreekvineyard.com*.

Healdsburg Town Square

Take a stroll around the square for a change of pace. It's loaded with quality shops.

Rodney Strong Vineyards

The main building features modern architecture outside and an educational, self-guided tour inside, adjacent to the tasting room. Be sure to see the panel featuring Sonoma County's winegrowing history from 1810 to 1990. An interesting fact: Rodney Strong uses the largest number of solar panels of any winery in the world. Try the Russian River Pinot Noir, Merlot, Meritage, and Sauvignon Blanc. Open daily 10am-5pm; 11455 Old Redwood Highway, Healdsburg 95448; 707-431-1533; *www.rodneystrong.com*.

To get to Korbel from Rodney Strong, take Old Redwood Hwy. and Eastside Rd. south to Wohler Rd., cross the river, then turn left onto Westside Rd. It's worth the drive.

Korbel Champagne Cellars

America's #1 champagne-maker is also known for its garden and winery tours. The Antique Rose Garden Tours are conducted mid-April through mid-October, Tuesday through Sunday, at 11am, 1pm and 3pm. The Champagne Cellar Tours (includes the champagne-making process and tasting) depart Monday through Friday at one-hour intervals between 10am and 3:45pm, and on Saturday and Sunday at 45-minute intervals between 10am and 3:45pm. Open for tasting daily 9am-5pm, except 9am-4:30pm October through April. Try the Korbel Brut and Korbel's wines and brandies. 13250 River Rd., Guerneville, 95446, 707-824-7000; *www.korbel.com*.

A Special Ocean-Front Dining Experience

If you're up to a little more driving, continue west along the scenic Russian River (via Westside Dr. and Highway 116), to Highway 1, then north about a half-mile to the River's End Restaurant in Jenner. You'll enjoy both an exceptional meal and a great view from a bluff overlooking the Pacific Ocean. Open daily 5-9pm during the summer and 5-9pm Thursday through Monday during spring and fall; 11048

Highway 1, Jenner 95450; 707-865-2484, Ext. 111; *www.ilovesunsets.com.* (Personal checks are not accepted.)

River's End also has rustic cabin accommodations, which can be reserved at the same telephone number.

Appendices

What to Wear, What to Bring

For Your Health and Safety

Geography, Weather, Facts, History, and Visitor Centers

If You Have Kids Along

Selected Readings

.

What to Wear, What to Bring

We have four suggestions (born of experience) about packing. First, be prepared for the season and be ready to put on or take off layers of clothing as necessary. Second, pack as little as possible; most people take more clothing than they need and end up hauling too many heavy suitcases. Third, consider using smaller suitcases with wheels and pull-handles. And, fourth, here is a list of particularly important things, some of which you might not think to bring along:

- A warm jacket, heavy sweater or sweatshirt, and long pants for the higher elevations and cool nights
- Light-weight long pants for protection while hiking in wooded areas
- Rain gear, including slickers and/or light-weight raincoats/jackets, and umbrellas
- Comfortable walking or hiking shoes that have been well broken-in
- A wide-brim hat and sunglasses with ultra-violet protection, because the sun (and UV) is more intense in the mountains.
- A camera and plenty of film or digital space, to capture those special scenes, animals or moments (if you use film, buy a lead-lined pouch at a camera store to pack it in, and put it in your carry-on bag, to avoid damage by airport scanners)
- Binoculars, especially to see wildlife or scenery up close
- A small first aid kit, to take care of potential blisters, cuts, headaches, colds and heartburn, plus a thermometer and tweezers
- Prescription medications, plus physician names and telephone numbers
- Telephone numbers of other emergency contacts (family and friends); also, leave your itinerary/phone (including cell phone) numbers with them
- A needle and thread, for emergency clothing repairs
- A pocket or Swiss Army knife with a can opener, also for emergencies (if you fly to California, this must be put in checked baggage)
- A flashlight with fresh batteries, to help you get around at night in unfamiliar surroundings
- A compass, insect repellent, sun screen, lip salve, matches, toilet paper, fanny pack, and canteen or water bottle, if you plan to hike
- Dress-up clothes, if you intend to dine in upscale restaurants; otherwise, you won't need them.

For Your Health and Safety

With a little knowledge and common sense you can prevent the health and safety problems that could spoil a great vacation. Only a small percentage of travelers experience these problems; we don't want you among them. Again we offer our mothers' admonition, "Forewarned is forearmed!" We are not doctors, but this accumulated wisdom that we've compiled from various sources and our own experience may be helpful.

Alcohol, in the form of wine, could slow your reflexes as you "taste the grape" in the Wine Country. *Prevention*: eat something between tastings and drive with care, or appoint a designated driver.

Altitude sickness, also known as acute mountain sickness, is caused by decreasing atmospheric pressure. That is, the higher you go in the mountains, the harder your heart, lungs, and body tissues must work to draw in oxygen. Symptoms include: a hammering headache, nausea, dizziness, fatigue, rapid heartbeat, shortness of breath, sleeplessness and loss of appetite.

Prevention: fast-walk, every day for 30 minutes, two to three weeks before you leave home. It's possible that you may experience one or more of the symptoms when you travel at higher locations such as Lake Tahoe. If you do feel ill, especially if you have heart or nervous system problems, stop immediately and descend more than 1,000 feet to a lower altitude. If your symptoms are mild, drink lots of water, rest awhile to give your body a chance to adapt, take the headache medicine that's in your first aid kit, avoid alcohol and cigarettes, and eat lightly and frequently.

Cardiac patients should consult with their doctors prior to the trip, and proceed with special caution in the mountains.

Dehydration, as you know, is excessive loss of water from the body tissues, which can cause fever, diarrhea, vomiting and acidosis. It can sneak up on you in California because the dry climate is so comfortable and water evaporates from the body more quickly. *Prevention*: increase your fluid intake (not alcohol), even when you don't feel thirsty.

Giardia, unlike dehydration, is something you may not have heard about. It's a microscopic organism found in lakes and streams which can cause diarrhea, cramps, bloating and weight loss. *Prevention*: don't drink the water in those crystal-clear streams and lakes—unless it's been boiled for at least five minutes or you use a water filter system that eliminates giardia.

Hypothermia is the lowering of the core body temperature to below 95 degrees F/35 degrees C, usually caused by prolonged exposure to cold and characterized by drowsiness, loss of judgment or coordination, slurred speech, uncontrolled shivering, cool and pale skin, and slowed pulse and breathing. *Prevention*: avoid prolonged exposure to cold; put on extra layers of clothing and the jacket, heavy sweater or sweatshirt you brought along—before you feel cold.

Sore leg muscles are a distinct possibility if you do any hiking. *Prevention*: start a conditioning regimen two or three weeks before you get to California; fast-walk 30 minutes or more every day, if your physical condition permits.

Sunburn is another familiar vacation spoiler. *Prevention*: wear a wide-brim hat, apply sunscreen and wear long sleeves and pants. And don't forget to wear those sunglasses! Potentially harmful ultra-violet rays are particularly strong at high elevations.

Ticks are abundant in early spring and summer throughout California. Some of them carry diseases such as Rocky Mountain spotted fever, Tularemia and Lyme's disease. *Prevention*: when hiking or walking through undergrowth, tuck your pant legs into your socks, treat clothing with insect repellent, and check daily for ticks. To remove an embedded tick, pull it out gently with tweezers, removing all head and neck parts to prevent infection.

Wildlife, especially bear, deer, and bighorn sheep in the mountains, are dangerous. *Prevention*: Keep a safe distance at all times. Do not feed them; doing so is not "a safe distance," and feeding them may make them aggressive. Also photograph all wildlife from a safe distance.

Here are some telephone numbers that may come in handy:

911 is an emergency number that you can dial anywhere in California. It will connect you with the nearest sheriff or police.

National Weather Service Forecast 831-656-1725 for San Francisco and Monterey; 559-584-3752 for the rest of Northern California; *www.weather.gov/sacramento*.

Road Conditions: 800-427-7623 for Northern California (within California only); 415-557-3755 for San Francisco; 209-372-0200 for Yosemite National Park; 530-542-4636 for South Lake Tahoe; 916-445-1534 for Sacramento.

Geography, Weather, Facts, History, and Visitor Centers

Northern California's Geography and Weather

Except for the Central Valley, Northern California is basically mountainous. To the north of the Valley are the Cascade and Klamath Mountains, to the west are two Coast Ranges, and to the east is the Sierra Nevada. The Sierras are the highest, with two mountains topping 14,000 feet (Whitney and North Palisade). The scenic standouts in the Sierras are Yosemite Valley and Lake Tahoe.

The Central Valley has two components: the Sacramento Valley in the north and the San Joaquin Valley in the south. The rivers that water them are the Sacramento and the San Joaquin. The entire valley is 450 miles long, extending into Southern California, and is about 50 miles wide. It is the most productive farming area in the United States.

The most "moving" area of Northern California is along the San Andreas Fault. It runs southeastward from Point Arenas into Southern California. The seaward side of the fault is moving northward at about two inches a year. When the fault moves, it's called an earthquake.

With such a diverse geography comes a wide range of climates. In general, however: temperatures and rainfall are mild along the coast; the Sierra Nevada has cold temperatures and heavy snowfall during the winter; and the Central Valley is hot and dry during the summer.

Some California Facts

- *Statehood*: September 9, 1850 (31st state)
- *Capitol:* Sacramento
- *State motto*: Eureka (I have found it)
- *Nickname:* The Golden State
- *Area*: 163,696 square miles (third largest state behind Alaska and Texas)
- *Coastline*: 840 miles
- *Population*: 35,480,000 (2003 estimate; largest in U.S.)
- *Bird*: California valley quail
- *Flower*: Golden poppy
- *Tree*: California redwood
- *Primary industries*: agriculture, tourism, apparel, electronics, telecommunications, entertainment
- *Primary manufactured goods*: electronic and electrical equipment, computers, industrial machinery, transportation

equipment and instruments, food
- *Primary farm products*: milk, grapes, cotton, flowers, oranges, rice, nursery products, hay, tomatoes, lettuce, strawberries, almonds, asparagus
- *Time Zone:* Pacific
- *Web site*: *www.state.ca.us*

Key Historical Events
- *Pre-1579*: More than 100 different tribes of mostly Hupa, Maidu, Quechan, Pomo, Miwok, Modic, and Mojave Indians occupied what was to become the State of California.
- *1579*: English sea captain Sir Francis Drake explored California's coast.
- *1602*: Spanish explorer Sebastian Vizcaino named many coastal landmarks.
- *1769 and 1770*: Captain Gaspar de Portola established the first military presidios at San Diego and Monterey.
- *1769-1821*: Franciscan friars established a chain of 21 missions stretching from San Diego to Sonoma.
- *1776*: a group of Spanish settled in Yerba Buena, now called San Francisco.
- *1812*: The Russians established Fort Ross (70 miles north of San Francisco) to support their sea otter fur trade.
- *1822*: Mexico won its independence from Spain and takes over "Alta (Upper) California."
- *1826*: Having crossed the southwestern deserts, trapper-explorer Jedediah Strong Smith was the first American to arrive in Mexican-controlled California.
- *1841*: A group of American settlers led by John Bidwell and John Bartleson arrived, also by land.
- *1844*: American military explorer, John C. Fremont, made his first reconnaissance of California.
- *1846*: Fremont made his second reconnaissance; the United States went to war with Mexico; a band of Americans captured Mexico's northern California headquarters in Sonoma (known as the Bear Flag Revolt); US Navy Commodore Drake Sloat raised the American flag over Monterey, claiming California for the U.S.
- *1848*: The U.S.-Mexican war ended; Mexico ceded California in the Treaty of Guadalupe Hidalgo.
- *1848*: John Marshall discovered Gold in the Sierra foothills

northeast of Sacramento.

- *1850*: California became the 31st state.
- *1865-1869*: The transcontinental railroad was built across the Sierra Nevada Mountains.
- *1906*: 28,000 buildings were destroyed and 3,000 people were killed in the great San Francisco earthquake.

Visitor Centers

- California Division of Tourism, P.O. 1499, Sacramento 95812, 800-GOCALIF, *http://gocalif.ca.gov*
- Carmel Chamber of Commerce & Visitor Information Center, San Carlos between 5th & 6th, P.O. Box 4444, Carmel 93921, 831-624-2522, 800-550-4333, *www.carmelcalifornia.org*
- Columbia Chamber of Commerce, P.O. Box 1824, Columbia 95310, 209-588-9128, *www.columbiacalifornia.com*
- Healdsburg Chamber of Commerce & Visitors Bureau, 217 Healdsburg Ave., Healdsburg 95448, 707-433-6935, *www.healdsburg.org*
- Lake Tahoe Visitors Authority, 1156 Ski Run Blvd., South Lake Tahoe, 96150, 530-544-5050, *www.virtualtahoe.com*
- Monterey County Convention & Visitors Bureau, P.O. Box 1770, Monterey 93942, 888-221-1010, *www.montereyinfo.org*. Or, local office: Monterey Visitors Center, Lake El Estero at Franklin & Camino El Estero, Monterey 93940, 888-221-1010
- Napa Valley Conference & Visitors Bureau, 1310 Napa Town Center, Napa 94559, 707-226-7459, *www.napavalley.com*
- Placerville: El Dorado County Chamber of Commerce, 542 Main St. Placerville 95667, 530-621-5885 or 800-457-6279, *www.eldoradocounty.org/visitor*
- Sacramento Convention & Visitors Bureau, 1303 "J" St., Suite 600, Sacramento 95814, 916-264-7777, 800-292-2334, *www.discovergold.org*
- San Francisco Convention & Visitors Bureau, 900 Market St., San Francisco 94103, 415-283-0177, *www.sfvisitor.org*
- Sonoma Valley Visitors Bureau, 453 First St. E., Sonoma 95476, 707-996-1090, *www.sonomavalley.com*
- St. Helena Chamber of Commerce, 1010 Main St., Suite A, St. Helena 94574, 800-799-6456, 707-963-4456, *www.sthelena.com*
- Yosemite Valley Visitor Center, Yosemite National Park, 209-372-0298, *www.nps.gov/yose*

If You Have Kids Along

You may want to look at one or more of these five books before you leave. All are included in the Selected Readings appendix of this book. Most recommend kid-friendly and family-priced restaurants and accommodations.

- *Around San Francisco With Kids: 68 Great Things to Do Together*
- *Frommer's San Francisco With Kids*
- *Fun With the Family in Northern California*
- *Insiders' Guide to the Monterey Peninsula* (includes a Kidstuff chapter)
- *The Unofficial Guide to California With Kids*

For example, *Fun With the Family in Northern California* recommends the following activities (among others) as good for kids. They are activities that we feature or mention in this book. *In other words, just bring the kids along; they'll enjoy the entire tour!*

San Francisco
- Alcatraz
- Cable Cars
- Cable Car Museum
- California Academy of Sciences
- Coit Tower
- The Exploratorium
- Fisherman's Wharf
- Hyde Street Pier and Maritime National Historical Park
- Maritime Museum
- Mission Dolores
- Pier 39
- The Presidio
- The San Francisco Museum of Modern Art

Monterey, Carmel and Nearby
- 17-Mile Drive
- Carmel Mission
- Monterey Bay Aquarium
- Monterey State Historic Park "Path of History"
- National Steinbeck Center (Salinas)
- Pfeiffer Beach (Big Sur)

- Point Lobos State Reserve
- Santa Cruz Beach Boardwalk

Yosemite National Park
- All of Yosemite Valley (including the Visitor's Center)
- Glacier Point
- Mariposa Grove
- Pioneer Yosemite History Center

Gold Country
- Calaveras Big Trees State Park
- Calaveras County Historical Museum
- Columbia State Historic Park
- Indian Grinding Rock State Historic Park
- Railtown 1897 State Historic Park

Tahoe
- D.L. Bliss State Park
- Donner Memorial State Park
- Heavenly Valley Tram
- Tahoe Queen Paddle wheeler
- Tallac Historic Site
- U.S. Forest Service Visitor's Center (Taylor Creek)

Sacramento
- California State Capitol
- California State Indian Museum
- California State Railroad Museum
- Old Sacramento State Historic Park
- Sutter's Fort

Wine Country and Nearby
- Benziger Family Winery
- Chateau Montelena
- Culinary Institute of America
- Dry Creek General Store
- Fort Ross State Historical Park (north of Jenner)
- General M.G. Vallejo Home
- Jack London State Park
- Sonoma Mission & Sonoma Barracks
- Sterling Vineyards

Selected Readings

If your library and bookstores are like ours, the shelves are filled with books on California. And Amazon.com is similarly well stocked. (Except for two of the following books, all are available on Amazon.com). The intention of this list is to help you narrow down the choices to books that we think will nicely supplement ours. Copyright dates are as of the publication of this book; most of these books are updated frequently.

Historical Books
This list is for those who like to dig into the history of an area before traveling.

- **California: A History,** by Andrew F. Rolle, Harlan Davidson, Wheeling, IL, 6th edition, 2003. A good, comprehensive history.
- **California: A History of the Golden State,** by Warren A. Beck and David A. Williams, Doubleday & Co., Garden City, NY, 1972. Another good, comprehensive history.
- **The Central Valley: California's Heartland,** by Stephen Johnson, Gerald Haslam and Robert Dawson, The University of California Press, Berkeley and Los Angeles, CA, 1993. A photo history.
- **El Dorado: The California Gold Rush,** by Dale L. Walker, Forge Books, New York, NY, 2003. The stories, people and events behind the era's headlines.
- **Historic Spots in California,** by Douglas E. Kyle and Mildred Brooke Hoover, Stanford University Press, Stanford, CA 2002. Bite-size histories by locality.
- **Nothing Like It in the World: The Men Who Built the Transcontinental Railroad 1863-1869,** by Stephen E. Ambrose, Simon & Schuster, 2001. A very interesting and excellently-written account that was used as a resource for Day Five and Day Six of this book.
- **Sacramento,** by William M. Holden, Two Rivers Publishing Co., Fair Oaks, CA 1988. Interestingly-written detail and anecdotes from Sacramento's past. An important resource for Day Six of this book. (Available only from the publisher or the Visitor Center and Discovery Museum in Old Sacramento.)

Travel Books

- **Adventure Guide to Northern California**, by Lee Foster and Mary Lou Janson, Hunter Publishing, Walpole, MA, 1998. A comprehensive guide which also includes adventure options such as bicycling, rafting, ballooning, hiking, and horseback riding.
- **Around San Francisco With Kids: 68 Great Things to Do Together**, by Clark Norton, Fodor's Travel Publications, New York, NY, 2002. Pocket size, separate text for parents and kids, "Eats for Kids" in each location.
- **California's Best-Loved Driving Tours**, Frommer's-Wiley Publishing, New York, NY 2005. Color photographs and details on 25 itineraries in eight areas of the state.
- **California Wine Country: The Napa and Sonoma Valleys—and Beyond**, by John Doerper, Compass American Guides, New York, NY, 2004. Great photographs and descriptions.
- **Coastal California**, by John Doerper, Compass American Guides, New York, NY, 2005. Describes the coast in bite-size segments: flora, fauna, history, food, lodging, wineries. Beautiful color photos.
- **The Complete Guidebook to Yosemite National Park**, by Steven P. Medley, The Yosemite Association, P.O. Box 320, El Portal, CA 95318, 2004. It is complete; the best single reference we've seen on Yosemite, in a handy size.
- **Fodor's Northern California**, Fodor's, New York, NY, 2006. Itineraries, maps, restaurants, lodging.
- **Foghorn Outdoors, California Camping: The Complete Guide to More Than 1,500 Campgrounds**, by Tom Stienstra, Avalon Travel Publishing, Emeryville, CA, 12th edition, 2003.
- **Frommer's San Francisco With Kids**, by Noelle Salmi, Frommer's/Wiley Publishing, New York, NY, 2005. Exploring, entertainment, side trips, family-friendly accommodations and dining.
- **Fun With the Family in Northern California**, by Karen Misuraca, Globe Pequot Press, Guilford, CT, 2004. Wonderful companion book to have along with ours; describes activities, where to eat and stay.
- **Insider's Guide to California's Wine Country**, by Jean

Saylor Doppenberg, Globe Pequot Press, Guilford, CT, 2003. A great resource for lodgings and restaurants.

- **Insiders' Guide to the Monterey Peninsula**, by Tom Owens and Melanie Bellon Chatfield, Globe Pequot Press, Guilford, CT 2004. History, attractions, shopping, accommodations, restaurants, nightlife, kid stuff, annual events, galleries, parks, day trips.
- **Let's Go California**, St. Martins Press, New York, NY, 2004. A comprehensive guide with good maps and descriptions.
- **Michelin Green Guide California**, Michelin Travel Publications, Greenville, SC, 2003. Maps, attractions well described and rated.
- **Mobil Travel Guide: Northern California 2006**, Exxon Mobil Travel Publications, Lincolnwood, IL, 2005. Attractions, special events, restaurants, and lodging.
- **Northern California Handbook**, by Kim Weir, Avalon Travel Publishing, Emeryville, CA, 2004. History, sights, accommodations, other practicalities.
- **Northern California & Nevada Tour Book**, AAA Publishing, Heathrow, FL 2006. Where to stay and where to dine, with ratings, by geographic area and town. (Available only through the American Automobile Assoc.)
- **Tahoe**, by Ken Castle, Foghorn Press, San Francisco, CA, 1995. A very comprehensive resource.
- **Top 10 San Francisco**, by Jeffrey Kennedy, DK Publishing, New York, NY, 2004. The author's favorite areas, features, museums, parks, bars, beaches, etc.
- **The Unofficial Guide to California With Kids**, by Colleen Dunn Bates and Susan La Tempa, John Wiley & Sons, New York, NY, 2005. Lists family-friendly restaurants and lodging; rates attractions' appeal by age group.
- **Woodall's North American Campground Directory**, Globe Pequot Press, Guilford, CT 2006. Campground listings with site-specific details.

Also by Bill and Celia Ginnodo
Seven Perfect Days in Colorado: A Guided Driving Tour

Their books can be viewed at
www.pridepublications.com
www.amazon.com (United States)
www.amazon.ca (Canada)
www.amazon.co.uk (United Kingdom)
www.bn.com (Barnes & Noble)
www.borders.com (Borders)

You'll find links to most of the tour's attractions and establishments at
www.pridepublications.com

Learn about the authors at
www.pridepublications.com

We would appreciate your feedback
Was this seven-day tour everything that you hoped for?
Are there things that should be improved in future printings?
Please contact us at *ginnodo@pridepublications.com*, 847-398-6212 (phone), 847-398-0670 (fax), or 4 N. Wilshire Lane, Arlington Heights, IL 60004